LETTERS AND ~~.~~ GS OF EPICURUS

Epicurus

Translation, Introduction, and Notes
by Odysseus Makridis

**BARNES
& NOBLE
BOOKS**

NEW YORK

CONTENTS

INTRODUCTION

THROUGHOUT the ages Epicurus (341–271 BCE) has been both idealized and anathematized. As an atheist materialist philosopher he was an offense to religious thinkers. Many of his influential admirers, like Thomas Hobbes and Thomas Jefferson, had to keep their Epicurean leanings a secret. On the other hand, the philosopher-physicist Isaac Newton was candid enough to assert openly that he was reviving the tenets of the Epicurean philosophy when he embarked on his world-transforming project. But Epicurus' significance transcends even his astounding historical influence because the subjects he reflected on are of enduring significance: What is the purpose of life? What is the nature of reality? How did this world come into existence? Is it going to last forever? How many worlds exist? What is the appropriate method for the investigation of natural phenomena? What are the proper criteria for establishing whether a claim is true or false? How should we live our lives? Should we fear death?

Epicurus' Life and Significance as a Thinker

Epicurus was born, probably in Athens, in 341 BCE. The city was a pale reflection of its resplendent past. The apogee of Sophocles' and Plato's golden age was now a pallid memory. The bustling cultural activity of Athenian life had waned irrevocably. Nevertheless, philosophy was by no means moribund. A remarkable trend was being set, which was destined later to continue and endure even under the auspices of the Roman Empire:

The allure of philosophy would prove irresistible for many vulgar newcomers. When we study other historical periods and cultures we find that the upstart is more likely to be attracted to conspicuous consumption of the garish sort. Remarkably, in the days of Epicurus and, even more so in Roman times, the ability to afford philosophic training was considered one of the most irresistible displays of high status. This almost serendipitous phenomenon ensured that philosophic activity would continue unabated for many centuries and would register a remarkable influence on many nascent systems, including Christianity itself. But there is a catch.

The problems inherited from the generations of Plato and Aristotle were alive and well. Debates were animated and philosophic enthusiasm did not pass from the earth. On the other hand, however, in the centuries that followed, the traditional problems of philosophy were often discussed in an unoriginal, reiterative fashion and, often, simply for the sake of creating impressions or with a view to producing dry "encyclopedic" compilations. This is not unique to this period of course—and it might be eerily similar to periods with which we are more familiar. An additional phenomenon was the exponential and rapid growth of mystical preoccupations. One could argue that Plato had a pronouncedly mystic side to his thinking; but, while Plato's mysticism is a metaphysically transcendental position, the new mysticism was a crude and frightened superstition. Epicurus' significance becomes more evident when we mention that the atomist philosopher saw himself as the enemy of superstition and champion of—what we would call today—commonsense rationalist empiricism.

By this time, the democratic experiment of the Athenian polis had all but been forgotten. (Of course, many celebrated ancient philosophers, including Plato himself, were harshly critical of Athenian democracy.) Unmoored from the salutary influence of civic life and reduced to passive and harassed dependency, the common folks became enthusiastic recipients of paranormal fables and superstitious tales. The popular interest in astrological trumpery seems to have been insatiable. It also seems to have been the case that the endless supply of tabloid-like tales about punishing gods actually contributed to an exacerbation of the maddening fears that had made such stories popular in the first place. This must have been a melancholy era indeed. If we keep this in mind, we will not be surprised by Epicurus' insistence that the greatest ethical value in the universe—and, hence, the proper goal of a human life—is peace of mind. (His detractors thought or, at any rate, claimed that Epicurus took pleasure to be the highest moral value, which, of course, placed Epicurus in the infamous clan of hedonists and ensured that the term Epicureanism would obtain unflattering connotations for posterity.)

To return, for a moment, to the dimension of philosophic activity: We should keep in mind that the fragmentation of philosophical speculation into several "disciplines" is a late phenomenon. Even Newton thought of himself as, primarily, someone who was engaged in philosophy. Physics and, what we call today metaphysics, were one; and ethics was joined with them too. This union was thought to be harmonious and in accordance with the natural order of things. Natural philosophy was driving developments, even though the ethical problems—understood to comprise the meaning of life and the proper purposes of human activity—were generally declared to be the most important. Before Epicurus, the atomic theory had been formulated by Leucippus and Democritus; its presumed refutation, however, had behind it the growing and formidable authority of none other than Aristotle himself. Epicurus picked up this ongoing debate; he reinvigorated and made original contributions to the atomist persuasion and derived a full-bodied metaphysics [theory of reality], epistemology [theory of knowledge], and even methodology [akin to today's philosophy of science] from his natural philosophy of Atomism; the whole system was said to point, with impeccable logical consistency, to an aggregate of ethical corollaries and maxims which promised to secure a happy—i.e., imperturbable and tranquil— life for the followers of the system.

We see, therefore, that Epicurus both undertook to contribute to a philosophical-scientific debate of grave importance *and* offered to soothe and heal the anguish of his age. He took this to be natural and logically of one piece although a less sympathetic age—and, in his own times, his numerous traducers—would charge that Epicurus was a phony who, under the veneer of prestigious philosophic pretensions, aspired to be a populist guru, self-important master of devoted disciples, and vain founder and propagandizer of a quasi-religious order. But this is not fair to Epicurus. He might have succumbed to vanity and transports of grandeur, but, to his credit, he concentrated unflinchingly on the most difficult problems of philosophy and worked indefatigably to produce and synthesize reasonable answers. As for the populist appeals of his teachings, Epicurus seems to have thought sincerely that he was offering an invaluable service to his contemporaries by turning the light of reason against the obscurantist horrors of popular superstition and a false astrological theology. It is a great tribute to Epicurus that many modern thinkers, including Thomas Hobbes and perhaps Thomas Jefferson, fashioned their own work, at least in part, after Epicurus' brave struggle on behalf of enlightening science and against popular superstition.

Epicurus' parents, Neocles and Chaerestrata, were impecunious Athenians who joined a mission of economically driven colonists. They settled on the island of Samos, in the East Aegean Archipelago. Epicurus grew up on the island and turned to philosophy at a ripe, young age. According to a legend, Epicurus decided to pursue philosophic studies when he was only fourteen when he became frustrated at his teacher's failure to explain an obscure passage in Hesiod's *Theogony* about the primeval chaos. While on Samos, Epicurus studied with the Platonist Pamphilus.

In 321, Epicurus joined the Athenians who had been previously expelled from Samos and were now living in Colophon, Anatolia. It is reported that, in Colophon, Epicurus did not waste much time before he entered into acrimonious philosophical antagonism with a local mind, Nausiphanes of Teos. Those were times when disputes over a philosophic problem could arouse the most vitriolic hatred and lead to irreconcilable animosity. Indeed, the quarrel with Nausiphanes must have become quite ferocious. It is also in this period that Epicurus, for the first time, grew fond of developing details about how one ought to live so as to live consistently with the true philosophy. The Epicurean cult and the adoration of Epicurus as a sage-guru was already in the making. Epicurus might have encouraged and even promoted this devotion. His adversaries always underlined this side of Epicurus' life and found here ample fodder for gossip and polemics.

In 311, Epicurus moved to Mytilene, on the island of Lesbos, where he opened a school of philosophic teaching. It appears that rumors soon spread and aspersions were cast on Epicurus and his disciples; the charge of impiety was leveled. It is likely that Epicurus was forcibly expelled from Lesbos. In 310, he moved to Lampsacus, near the Hellespont, where he began to proselytize and teach. He lived in Lampsacus until 306 and, in this period, gained a substantial number of devoted students.

In 306, he moved to Athens with a few of his pupils. He was to remain in Athens for the rest of his life. He bought a house and the celebrated—or, dependent on which side refers to it, infamous— Garden. It was in this garden, in aloofness and behind high walls, that the philosophic cult of Epicurus waxed and thrived. It could be argued that Socrates had been the first Greek thinker who sensed that the stakes in philosophical debate are so high and philosophy's scope so encompassing that the philosopher's pursuit ought to be not simply an inquiry but a complete and engrossing way of life. Epicurus was putting this Socratic insight to practice and, given the tenor and prejudices of his times, he was compelled to carry on with his philosophic activities in splendid isolation, behind the fortifying walls of the notorious Epicurean Garden. Predictably, the outside world took a dim and hostile view of this insular and elitist cult. It must be said, however, that Epicurus considered the appeal of his philosophy to be unencumbered from any distinctions of class, background, race, or even gender. And, indeed, the content of his philosophy and its appeal to accessible common-sense empiricism are consistent with an ideology of political equality: It does not take exceptional natural character of mind to follow the Epicurean principles and precepts. To use A. E. Taylor's apt phrase, Epicurus' philosophy is "anti-elitist." The Epicurean system appeals to common sense, privileges the viewpoint of ordinarily and commonly available experience, and recommends a prudential approach to life's ethical challenges which is within everyone's reach. Epicurean materialism rejects the inequality of Platonic excellence insofar as it rejects excellence itself—every human being, including the presumably greatest ones, is simply an aggregate of self-organizing material particles. As shown by the political philosopher Leo Strauss, this egalitarian bent of Epicurean materialism was diagnosed and emulated by many modern thinkers; Thomas Hobbes based his own egalitarian social-contract theory on a resuscitated and partly revamped Epicureanism.

Few other thinkers have been treated to the relentless vituperation hurled at Epicurus both by his contemporaries and by critics throughout the ages. G. Panichas has anthologized the lurid epithets with which ancient sources on Epicurus teem: "a most shameless physicist"; "flatterer of authority"; "plagiarist of Democritus"; "teacher of effeminacy"; "nasty name-caller"; "writer of lewd letters." Rumors had Epicurus indulge in extravagant feasts and orgies. It was claimed that he would induce vomiting twice a day so that he could continue unobstructed in his bulimic excesses. It was also said that Epicurus believed in the potency of magical incantations—a preposterous charge, considering Epicurus' unequivocal condemnation of superstitious ritual. Other rumors claimed that his mother had been a magician—and that, as a boy, Epicurus had followed her around as her assistant; that his brother was a pimp; and that he lacked good taste altogether and had embarrassingly boorish habits.

In reality, the Epicurean Garden served as something of an institution for mutual assistance of the school's members. Life in the Garden was regulated on the basis of detailed pecuniary and sumptuary regulations and with a view to preventing mischief and encouraging trust. The value of friendship was stressed—although Epicurus' critics doubted that his utilitarian calculus could endorse true friendship. The students were exhorted to lead a life of modest and prudent pleasures and to shun unnecessary distractions and short-lived flamboyant satisfactions. Property was not shared—and the justification that is reported for this, rather unconvincingly if not contradictorily, is that Epicurus thought commonly owned property to be a source of distrust.

Epicurus urged his students to memorize the main points of his system and promised that following the system both by repeating its principles and by putting it to practice would ensure freedom from bodily, and especially from mental, distress. Epicurus found the religious tales about an afterlife to be the most forbidding obstacle to attaining a serene life and the most baneful source of dread. To make full sense of this, we need to realize that, in pre-Christian times, the Greek tales about the afterlife were replete with terror: Horrendous and eternal punishments were meted out to various nefarious characters but, at the same time, it was not always made clear how one came to merit such punishment, and the frightening possibility was entertained that one could become the victim of divine malice and be condemned without appeal or judicial remedy. (In Christian times, Calvinism, for reasons of its own, resurrected this spectrum, often with equally calamitous consequences of the average person's peace of mind.) Epicurus' contemporaries, like those of Socrates and Plato, took the gods to be fickle, vindictive, spoiled, malicious, and unjust—which was a consistent view since the gods were considered extremely powerful and it was also thought that one who has immense power is at liberty, and might have every good and selfish reason, to behave badly toward others. Plato had protested against the logical and ethical-philosophical inconsistencies of this view but, by the time of Epicurus, the nuances of Platonism, which was not intended for the masses anyway, were not available for the huddled masses. It is within this context that we must read Epicurus' claim that the supreme aim of his system is to secure peace of mind.

It is pivotal to Epicurus' promise that one accepts the atomist philosophy of nature. This does not mean that Atomism is taken to be a stopgap ad-hoc theory which is introduced for the sake of calming public terror. The atomic philosophy is seen as the true one, which, incidentally, once grasped, takes care of fear and anguish. Nevertheless, many thought that the tranquility promised by Epicurus is purchased at a prohibitive price: Epicurus' philosophy is materialism and, in spite of his professed belief in the existence of material divinities, essentially atheistic. That the philosophy is materialist would not have been an anathema to the ancients because natural philosophies had been materialist anyway. Indeed, an alternative to philosophic materialism did not have to be, and might not have been, conceived if it were not for the influence of the Orphic rites on Plato. Plato's philosophy argued for the existence of an immaterial soul—it may or may not be the case that Socrates had believed in the immortal immaterial soul. It is the immaterial soul that is immortal. The material body, or even a material soul like the one presented by Epicurus, is destined to succumb to the perennial natural law of decomposition. The horror of Platonists was that, if it were ever found out that the immortal soul does not exist and that eternal punishments are not to be feared, the whole world would degenerate into anarchic, nihilistic chaos. So, the confession in philosophic materialism was to be taken as a sign of dangerous radicalism. And, for obvious reasons, this was the position adopted by the Christian thinkers, and, one suspects, even those Christian writers who harbored inner doubts about faith and dogma thought that there was every good reason to disavow and condemn atheism in order to safeguard public morals. So, throughout the ages, atheist Epicureanism was preserved as a term of invective.

Epicurus died in 271. He refers to his fatal ailments as "strangury and dysentery"—painful, incomplete urination probably caused by a bladder obstruction. As we know from an extant letter, Epicurus was proud to be facing death with fearless equanimity. Diogenes Laertius, who has preserved for us the very few Epicurean texts we have, heaps praises on Epicurus: The philosopher was gentle, humane, simple in his manners, and reasonable in his outlook.

It was said that Epicurus' writings could fill an entire library room, but very little survives today. Our sources for Epicurus' philosophy—translated in this volume—are a few letters and a compendium of maxims. There are also fragments, which do not add much to our understanding of Epicurus' philosophy, and testimonia, some of which are of dubious authenticity. The two seminal texts on Epicurus' natural philosophy, including his methodology, are his "Letter to Herodotus" and "Letter to Pythocles." Epicurus' ethical teachings are contained in his "Letter to Menoeceus" and in a pithy collection of maxims known as "Principal Doctrines." An excavation in the twentieth century produced one more text, the so-called "Vatican Sayings" which has not been included in the present selection as it corresponds very closely to the "Principal Doctrines." An excellent and elaborate source on Epicurus' philosophy, which we still have with us, is from Roman times: A devoted student of Epicurus, Lucretius, wrote a poem, *de rerum natura* (*On the Nature of the Universe*), which refers to, and often gives considerable details about, many Epicurean theories, including some that are not mentioned at all in the extant writings of Epicurus.

Epicurus' Philosophic System

The dispute between the Epicureans, on the one hand, and the Platonists and Neoplatonists, on the other, raged for centuries. Roughly, Epicurus and his disciples anticipated what we know today as a hard-hewn, no-nonsense, anti-mystical, pro-empiricist approach while the Platonists and Neoplatonists, encouraged by Plato's own writings and abetted by times of distress and upheaval, defended the claims of consolatory mysticism and opted for speculative flights into transcendental epistemologies. Epicurus' philosophical system even anticipated such recent developments in philosophy and science as the logical-positivist emphasis on a criterion of verification of truth claims, the scientific-methodological test of falsifiability of hypotheses, and the conventionalist demand for unambiguous operational definition of crucial terms. Equally impressive is Epicurus' close anticipation of Newtonian physics. Perhaps, the correct way of putting this is the other way round: It is a lasting testament to Epicurus' significance that, as generally acknowledged, Newton was able to formulate his system by rejecting the medieval-Aristotelian plenum and by reviving the ancient Epicurean claim of the existence of empty space.[1] In political thought, Epicurus anticipated contractarianism. In ethics, he managed to eke out a set of moral imperatives for the good life even though, once again anticipating the late nineteenth and twentieth centuries, he seems to have diagnosed a failure on the part of authoritatively prescriptive ethics to find secure foundations.

Like Newton's physics, Epicurus atomist philosophy is anti-teleological. The Aristotelian system, which was destined later to dominate the thought of the Middle Ages, is a typically teleological system: The distinctive feature of teleology is that it considers nature to be purposeful. The highest form of cause in the Aristotelian system is the so-called final cause: The goal or purpose for the sake of which objects are actualized. In the same way that the wood and the carpenter's effort are ancillary causes to the main purposive intent of creating a piece of furniture, so does intelligent Nature operate causally on the basis of structured and meaningful purposes. This view is not conducive to experimentation because one would be better off using his or her mind to read the book of nature and because, at any rate, the discovery of irregularities and errors would not advance knowledge under this system: Failures are considered to be freakish occurrences which violate the wisdom of natural order rather than occasions for further investigation. Epicurus rejected Aristotelian teleology. According to Epicurus' atomic theory, motion is not a providentially directed activity or purpose-guided transition into actuality but a brute fact. The atomic composition of everything ensures that nature is ultimately self-organizing but also that this self-organization is blind and random. Since the atom is not rational, Epicurus' principle of natural self-organization is indeed a concession that nature is ruled by chance rather than intelligent purpose. Epicurus' courage in claiming that the atom—an unintelligent and basic entity—has inherent motion can be appreciated better by realizing that similar claims, raised by certain variants of chaos theory, are considered radical even today. Epicurus' radicalism in this respect outpaces even the mechanistic model of the Enlightenment, which is still congenial to common sense. The Enlightenment model of a mechanistic universe leaves space for an intelligent blueprint behind the machinery, whereas Epicurus' atomic theory, rightly understood, does not.

Epicurus produced his theory inspired by the ancient atomists Leucippus and Democritus. Like all ancient thinkers, Epicurus reached his conclusions by using only reasoning. It is remarkable, however, that Epicurus seems to have been obsessed with the deepest questions of method and what we would consider today philosophy of science. Even his brief extant summaries, which are explicitly intended to serve as synopses and for the purpose of memorization, do not resist laying stress on methodological matters. Here are some of Epicurus' methodological principles: The testimony of the senses is the ultimate arbiter of disputes. One should not unnecessarily multiply assumptions if directly accessible experience affords us observation of phenomena similar to the remote and obscure ones we are trying to explain. We should not assume that only one explanation is available or that only one process might be at work in producing the phenomenon we are trying to account for; at the same time, we should make sure to reject explanations which cannot be confirmed at all and, especially, those which have empirical testimony against them. This last caveat is significant: Epicurus clearly placed extraordinary emphasis on what we could call today the verificationist criterion of truth. According to Epicurus, knowledge ultimately comes from empirical observation. Epicurus has the metaphysics to go with this claim: Everything we know, even including mental constructs and figments of the imagination, is ultimately produced by the same atomic constituents of which all the real objects in the universe are made.

The major difference between Democritus' and Epicurus' atomic theories is that Democritus had taken seriously the difference between the underlying atomic reality and the appearances which do not show us the atoms directly: This led Democritus to rationalism—the demand that we trust only our logical thinking, since we are able to reach the true atomic constitution of matter only by means of thinking and not by direct observation. Epicurus rejected this and opted for a robust empiricism on the grounds that our very thinking processes are ultimately produced by atoms anyway.

[handwritten marginal note: rationalism vs empiricism]

The impetus for the development of the original atomic theory might have been a number of paradoxes formulated by Zeno of Elea, which purported to show that motion is illusory. The paradoxes of Zeno, which have survived, exploit the geometrical claim that line segments, and indeed any measurable intervals, are infinitely subdivisible. If that is the case, anything that moves in space or time would have to move an infinite number of points between any two points—in current jargon, it would have to perform a supertask which involves undertaking an infinite number of actions and, therefore, can never be completed. The atomists countered that matter is not infinitely subdivisible. The ultimate constituents of matter are the atoms that are unbreakable. These may or may not be "minima" in terms of their sizes—after all, they might come in many different sizes—but they are certainly indivisible or uncuttable. Epicurus made it clear that different sizes of atoms exist, but he pointed out that this must be a finite number anyway. His argument to this effect deserves mention: If an infinite number of atomic sizes existed, then some of those sizes would inevitably be large enough to be visible; but the atoms are invisible. (There seems to have been some confusion on this score among the atomists, with some of them maintaining that certain atoms may indeed be visible to the naked eye.)

The atoms have only a limited number of fundamental properties—size, shape, and mass. Since the atoms have motion inherent to them, Epicurus did not think that he could differentiate atomic types on the basis of motion; he seems to have thought that atoms move with a standard velocity—perhaps something of a universal constant—and he seems to have compared this to another speed quantity to which he attached great significance—the speed of thought.

In addition to his atomic theory, Epicurus requests that the student accept one more principle: that empty space exists. This makes Epicurus what we could call today a Substantivalist: Epicurean space is somewhat like Newtonian absolute space—an infinite super-substance that exists on its own right. It seems that Epicurus considered empty space, known in antiquity as "the void," to be inert, its existence simply enabling movement. Epicurus thought that he had actually proved the existence of empty space—in other words, and strictly speaking, he did not offer this proposition as a postulate. His proof goes something like this: If empty space did not exist, bodies would not have anything through which they could move and, therefore, motion would be impossible. But motion is clearly possible. Therefore, empty space exists. A full appreciation of this, however, is possible only by taking into account Epicurus' rejection of Aristotle's plenum. Very little on this score is available in the extant writings of Epicurus.

Epicurus derives a number of corollaries that follow from his two basic principles—the atomic principle and the empty space principle.

Space is infinitely extended or unbounded. Epicurus provided, or repeated a formerly known, proof to this effect, in the form of a constructive dilemma: Let us walk to the edge of space, wherever that may be, and attempt to walk further. If we can always do this, then the process is infinitely repeatable and, therefore, space is infinitely extended. If we cannot do this, then we must be touching the veritable edge or boundary of the universe. But an edge or boundary is, by definition, touching on something else. From this definition of boundary, Epicurus thought that he could show that even if we come to a boundary there is more beyond the boundary and still more, for the same reason, beyond the new boundary, and so on ad infinitum. (A topographically available alternative to Epicurus', and later Newton's, view of the infinite extension of empty space is a spherical surface, which is unbounded but not infinitely extended. This is what Einstein opted for. Even in that case, we might wonder about the putative space wherein the supposed sphere is located, but modern physics shelves this question as unanswerable. The philosophical alternative to Epicurus-Newton is the rejection of a real external space: This can be done by means of Idealist and Relationist theories of space.)

Since space is infinitely extended, the number of atoms in the universe must be infinite too. Epicurus reaches this conclusion by applying an early version of what we call today the anthropic principle. Since it is obvious that the present world exists, it must be that the requisite processes for the formation of this world were enabled at some point in the past. But if only a finite number of atoms were moving throughout an infinitely extended space, then, Epicurus thinks, they could not have met to create the world in which we live. (Epicurus does not have a solid case here. The chances for the atoms to meet would indeed become vastly small but not zero; and the fact that we exist, and, hence, that our world, whatever this world is like, exists can be used as proof that the astronomically small chance the atoms had of meeting did indeed materialize.)

Even though an infinite number of atoms exists, according to Epicurus, the number of types of atoms is finite. Epicurus argues in favor of this by observing, as pointed above, that visible atoms would have to exist too if the variety of atomic types were infinite: because many—indeed, an infinite number—of atomic sizes would then have to lie above the visibility register. Hence, Epicurus concludes, the number of atomic types is finite; yet, it is vast because, otherwise, the astounding variety of things in our universe could not have come into existence.

Since worlds are created by the collisions and sorting of atoms and an infinite number of atoms are moving throughout an infinitely extended space, an infinite number of worlds exists. Our world is only one world. All these worlds are actual and coexist within the infinitely extended universe. Since worlds are formed accidentally and opportunistically, as it were, they can continue to form when the appropriate conditions are available. Moreover, the worlds are not permanent or eternal. Only the atoms are indestructible. Everything else is liable to dissolve unto its constituent components. Given enough time, the worlds too perish while other worlds are constantly being created. Some worlds are like our own but nothing precludes the possibility that dramatically different worlds exist—indeed, since we are dealing with an infinity of worlds, worlds different from ours must exist. On the other hand, given the fact that the number of atomic types is limited, there must also be a limit to the number of types of worlds that exist.

The soul is composed of exceedingly refined or fine-grained atoms. The person or self is the union of the body and the soul. The conscious person is the real person and this consciousness requires both body and the more refined, but still material, soul operating together. The soul is scattered throughout the body, by virtue of its refined material constitution, although it might be more partially associated with certain regions of the body. All this can explain why loss of limbs does not necessarily entail cessation of consciousness or life insofar as the soul is unaffected. On the other hand, however, if the body were gravely afflicted, the soul could not continue to exist by itself. Hence, there is no immortality. Epicurus thinks that this is good news: Most people, he observes, are terrified by the prospects of torments in an afterlife; and they dread the prospect of death itself. But there is no afterlife for the soul if the soul itself is not immortal. And, as for death, Epicurus has an argument that is renowned and has been repeated in various forms by twentieth-century thinkers like Jean Paul Sartre. This argument purports to show that death "is nothing to us" as Epicurus puts it. If death is defined, as it should be defined, as the discontinuation of the union of body and soul and consequent destruction of the individual, then there is no one there to experience his or her own death. The moments leading to death, when the person is still present, do not constitute death of the person properly speaking. So, death is never experienced and dread of death is illogical—it is, indeed, the very model of an illogical phobia insofar as it has literally nothing for its object. Epicurus needs more premises, which he supplies obligingly: Nature has contrived to ease the pain we feel, even when we are terminally afflicted with disease. Pains are never severe, or they are no longer experienced, Epicurus thought, when they surpass a certain threshold. Countervailing pleasures are available and, somehow, the dialectic of pain and pleasure is in our favor. Although Epicurus' nature is not teleological, as was pointed out above, nature has accidentally equipped us with what we need and furnished us with what it takes in order to render life enjoyable or, at least, bearable. Epicurus is not convinced by those who lament life and taunts them: If they have persuaded themselves that life is so bad, Epicurus charges, why don't they kill themselves? The final solution would be easy because distress of mind is more formidable than pain of the body, according to Epicurus: So, if someone has endured the ordeal of the proof of life's worthlessness and intolerable painfulness, then the remaining step, of causing one's death, is trivial. The fact that death-lovers are clinging to life proves to Epicurus either that they have not proved what they think they did or that they are blatant hypocrites.

 Epicurus professes to believe in the existence of gods who are composed of exceedingly fine-grained atoms. It is not clear why those gods would be immortal, as Epicurus wants them to be, since only atoms are indestructible in Epicurus' philosophy. Perhaps this is a telltale sign that Epicurus' references to the gods are not sincere. At any rate, Epicurus' gods are aloof and do not play any morally or historically significant role in human affairs. Epicurus tries to occupy the high moral ground in this respect, charging that those who burden gods with human affairs are guilty of impiety because they drag the divine down into the morass of human wretchedness and, on top of that, they are essentially depicting gods as irrational or wicked since only a fool would voluntarily abandon eternal bliss for the yoke of supervising human rewards and punishments and only a villain would give up aloofness and tranquility to gloat over human tragedies.

It seems that Epicurus was concerned about the deterministic implications of his philosophy. We don't hear about this in his extant writings but his Roman admirer Lucretius has preserved extensive information on this issue. Since events are simply due to atoms colliding, bouncing, and being sorted out, there is no space for human freedom left. This seems intuitively clear although, on closer inspection, it is not obvious why freedom should be preserved even if nature were unpredictable and non-deterministic or chaotic (in the traditional sense of the term chaotic.) But perhaps the absence of strict or sweeping determinism is the necessary, even if not sufficient, condition for human freedom. Even so, a view that is firmly committed to human freedom runs against a problem: One must assume that there is a. . .truly free person behind the guided person—the notorious "homunculus" hypothesis. Someone must be free to steer my actions and this free person, to be truly free, should not be "guided" by anything—including the gathering and parting concourses of atoms which determine all events according to materialism. I cannot go into additional details here but Epicurus apparently took this seriously and tried to preserve human freedom by undermining the strict-determinism premise. Although the atoms do indeed follow the inexorable impetus provided by their properties—mass, size, shape—there is a qualification to this. The atoms can only move downward, under the thrust of their mass (there is no weight-inducing gravitational field for Epicurus), or in the direction in which they bounce off after they happen to collide with other atoms. Epicurus must have thought that the latter direction is always horizontal. At any rate, oblique trajectories have to be composites of a finite number of infinitesimal vertical (mass-induced) and horizontal (collision-induced) trajectories, as Walter Englert concluded in his valuable study of this subject. This is still deterministic, though. Epicurus claimed that the vertical trajectory is not straight and inexorable: As they fall downward, the atoms swerve. Epicurus thought that this solves two problems for his theory: It accounts for human freedom insofar as events are, at least in part, unpredictable due to the unforeseeable and random swerve of atoms; and the swerve hypothesis makes his account of the genesis of worlds more plausible, Epicurus thought, insofar as the swerve makes it more likely that atoms will indeed meet and collide.

Epicurus' ethics posits the proposition that nature has determined what the good consists in. As ample evidence demonstrates, pleasure and the avoidance of pain, which regulate the behaviors of humans and animals, are what natural good consists in. Epicurus, like so many others both in ancient and in modern times, commits what G. E. Moore called the "naturalistic fallacy" in not realizing that one must already somehow know what the ethical meaning of "good" is before one can confidently establish that this or that—for instance, pleasure—is morally good. Epicurus' ethical theory is a strain of hedonism; it is not like the utilitarianism of modern times because Epicurus does not demand that moral agents act to maximize the greatest happiness of the greatest number of people. On the other hand, however, it is not fair to Epicurus to compare his ethical theory to any of the vulgar versions of self-centered and excessive hedonism with which the term Epicurean is often associated. Epicurus' theory claims a noble concern with living a life of dignity and tranquility. Natural pleasures are classified according to nature and in accord with whether they are necessary or not and the student is exhorted to abstain from unnecessary and frivolous pleasures. Epicurus must have run into trouble, philosophically speaking, by waffling as to whether pleasure consists in an active state or simply in the removal of pain and the supervening passive state of imperturbable serenity. His classification of pleasures into dynamic and static did not alleviate this problem; commentators fought mightily over whether the nature of pleasure itself consists in a dynamism inherent to the right kind of effort or in the peace of mind and muscular relaxation that naturally follow satisfaction of needs.

pleasure

Finally, Epicurus conceived of a contractarian theory of society. Crucial to this is the claim that, contrary to what Aristotle had claimed, the human being is not a sociable animal. Essentially, this forestalls an ethic of excellence because Aristotelian excellence is something that can flourish and be recognized only in a social arena; and, if humans are not sociable by nature, excellence itself cannot be what nature intended. It follows that, by nature, human beings were meant for the simplest tasks: following their natural instincts in seeking pleasure until they satisfy their needs and striving to avoid pain by all means. A radicalization of the egalitarian impetus of this theory by such formidable figures as Thomas Hobbes and John Locke gave us the theories of social justice and legitimacy, which culminated in the American Declaration of Independence and the classical-liberal view of the minimal state and the separation of civic society from the arena of private achievement. Unlike John Locke, Epicurus did not see fit to derive an ethical theory directly from his claims about the contractarian origin of civil society. It is not even clear how citizens would be compelled to keep the implicit promise they are presumed to have given in the moment of the formation of society. This has been a contested point and occasionally an embarrassment for modern contractarian theory. It is plausible that there is an interesting Epicurean solution to this problem: If one were to follow Epicurus' ethical advice and retreat behind the Garden, there to practice prudent uses of pleasures and live in aloofness, then citizens could hardly pose challenges or threats to public order and stability. It underscores, once again, the significance of Epicurus to note that this is one of the first *moral* arguments which, scandalously from the viewpoint of

Conformism

individualism

antiquity, advocates leading a private and secluded life. As Epicurus liked to put it, a principal moral maxim is: "Pass your life making sure no one notices you."

Odysseus Makridis received his Ph.D. from Brandeis University. He is Assistant Professor of Philosophy at Fairleigh Dickinson University, in Madison, New Jersey.

A NOTE ON THE TRANSLATION

IDENTIFICATION and titles of sections are provided by the translator. <> signifies translator's gloss, inserted, as needed, to make the test intelligible; the remarks inserted are understood as being implied by the text.
{} signifies a reconstruction of missing or unclear text.
*** signifies a lacuna in the text.

References designated by the capital letter U are to Hermann Usener, editor, Epicurea (Leipzig: Teubner, 1887). The numerals following U refer to the numbers assigned to the text by Usener.

EPICURUS,

LETTER TO HERODOTUS

{Diogenes Laertius X.34–83}

FROM Epicurus to Herodotus: Greetings.

Prologue: The Purpose of this Epitome

For those, Herodotus, who are unable to figure out with precision each and every one of our writings on nature, and for those who are unable to read the longer of our compositions, one would do well to prepare an epitome of the whole treatment in order to make possible memorization of the most consummate teachings. In this way, <students> may be able, at all times and regardless of the vagaries of fortune, to help themselves by only retaining a firm grasp of this <summary> of the natural philosophy.

But even those who are sufficiently advanced in the comprehensive understanding of all the teachings must still make sure to commit to memory the elementary outline of the entire treatise <on Nature.>

Because the need to repair to the summary application of the theory arises all too often, which is not the case with partial and specific applications.

Statement on Methodology

One should indeed step back into these fundamental lessons time and again and etch them deeply into his memory. The most crucial applications of theory on concrete situations are

1

made possible thanks to memorization. It will also be possible always to discover particulars with greater precision after one has encompassed and memorized the most complete outline <of the theory.>

Because, even for one who has completed his studies successfully, the main test of precise knowledge is this: that he is able to make astute specific applications of the theory by referring everything properly to the elements of the system and by using simple, formulaic propositions.

Nor would it be possible to survey the whole dense array, such as it is, of the concatenated studies of all things, unless one were able to capture and hold everything by means of brief statements. And this applies also to all those things, which it is possible to study specifically and with precision.

Since this method is useful for all those who are familiar with the study of nature, and considering that I recommend the continuous pursuit of this study and find tranquility in such studies more than in anything else in my life, I have composed for your benefit such a summary outline and elementary presentation of all my teachings.

Methodological Statement on Language and Meaning

First, Herodotus, we need to have received the right teachings about all those things which are properly denoted by utterances; so that we can make correct judgments about the things about which people form opinions, inquire, and wonder. This we can do after we have referred all <subjects of inquiry> to meaningful utterances. And we need to do this in order to be able to offer judgment regarding things—something we would never be able to do if we entered in disputation that can never be terminated <because of the use of meaningless statements.> And we need to do this also simply in order to avoid uttering meaningless, empty statements.

It is necessary that the primary conceptual meaning of each word should be given and that this account should not need any additional demonstrative analysis in any respect. We need to do this if we are to have something, to which we can refer the subject about which we are inquiring, opining, or wondering.

Methodological Statement on Epistemic Limitations

Furthermore, we must always keep within the limits set by sense perception. More specifically, we must confine ourselves within the scope of whatever the current applications of our intelligence or some <meaningful> criterion allow. And, similarly, at all times we must keep within the limits set by what our current emotive impressions. In this way we can have a foundation that allows us to draw inferences both about what is not evident to the senses as well as about that subject at hand.

Having spelled out such preliminary points, we must next make sure to take a synoptic view of <what we mean by> non-evident.

The Whole (The Totality of Things)

First of all, we need to state that nothing comes into existence from what does not exist. Because, in that case, everything would <be able to> come into existence out of everything, having no need whatever of a specific seed.

And if what is destroyed were to vanish into what does not exist, all things would have destroyed <by now> considering that things would be dissolving into. . .non-existent things. Moreover, the totality of things has always been what it is now; and will always be the same. Because there is not a single thing into which it might change—no thing <can be said logically to> exist outside the whole. <And since there is no thing outside the whole, there is nothing that> could enter the whole and produce a change.

Natural Kinds

It is generally true that all things that exist are either bodies or empty space.

Sense perception itself attests that bodies exist. And, as I said previously, it is necessary to draw inferences about what is non-evident <to the senses> by using reasoning and by arguing from premises that are consistent with the testimony of sense perception.

If, on the other hand, empty space does not exist—and we call this empty space "void," "place," and "intangible nature"—the bodies would have no space where they could be; nor would they have a medium, through which they could move—and yet, they appear clearly to be in motion.

Besides these two kinds, <bodies and empty space,> it is impossible to conceive of anything else either by means of a comprehensive survey of everything we know or by drawing analogies to anything we have come to grasp through perception. This applies to all those things, which perceive and accept <as being in existence> by nature and as integral entities; it does not apply to those things, to which we refer as the "properties" and "accidental attributes" of beings.

And, as for bodies, there are two kinds: Some are composites and others are those from which the composites are made.

Atoms

The latter are indivisible and immutable. If such did not exist—that is, if some things did not perdure even when the composites have been dissolved—everything would have been destroyed and become no-being <by now.>

But <the atoms or indivisibles> cannot be dissolved because they are complete natures to begin with; and because they have no way for undergoing dissolution; and because there is nothing into which they could dissolve.

So it must be the case that the building blocks <and ultimate explanatory principles> of bodily natures are the atoms or indivisibles.

The Whole Has No Boundary

The whole is without boundary. For what is compassed by a boundary must have an edge beyond which there is nothing. But we can make only sense of and perceive an edge as being next to something else. Therefore, since it is impossible for it to have an edge, the whole is without boundary. So, not having any outer boundaries, the whole cannot be bound around; it follows that it is without boundary.

Infinite Number of Bodies and Infinite Space

Moreover, the whole is unlimited in terms of the number of bodies it contains and in terms of the size of the empty space in it.

Indeed, if the empty space were unlimited while the number of bodies was determinate, the bodies could not ever come to rest or abide anywhere; instead, they would be carried about all over the boundless empty space; therefore, they would have remained forever scattered about since there would be no overarching entity <to keep them together;> and they would <come across> nothing that could collide with them and pin them to a place.

Composition and Dissolution of Bodies

If, on the other hand, the empty space had a determinate size, an infinite number of bodies would not have had sufficient room for them to exist.

In addition, the indivisible components of bodies are also complete as they are. The compositions, <which are the bodily entities,> come to be from these atoms and the decompositions <of bodies> are dissolutions unto atoms.

The Shapes of Atoms

The number of the different shapes of the atoms is vast beyond expression. Because it is indeed impossible that such a variety <of visible bodies> would come to be by compassing the same <few> shapes.

And, corresponding to each <atomic> shape, there is an infinite number of similarly shaped atoms. But, with respect to the number of the different shapes of atoms—this number is not infinite but simply vast beyond expression.

The Motion and Vicissitudes of the Atoms

And the atoms are perpetually in motion throughout the vast ages *** some standing apart from each other and others continuing to maintain a coordinate vibration—which happens if they chance to swerve <from their initial trajectories> and become entangled of if they are "housed" by other atoms which have become entangled.

And it is the nature of the empty space that makes this happen by demarcating boundaries around each atom while at the same time it <the empty space> is unable to offer a supporting superstructure <which would hold the atoms together and restrict atomic movement.>

Moreover, the solidity that is inherent to the atoms results in a characteristic vibration in the opposite direction following a collision; this vibration has a value that depends on the intensity of the collision and carries the atom to a distance permitted by the consequent entanglement and until the initial conditions are restored.

And there is no absolute beginning of such motions, since both the atoms and the empty space have existed forever.

Methodological Statement

This lecture so far—if one were to commit it to memory—can supply an adequate model leading to an understanding of the natures of beings.

Infinite Number of Worlds

And the number of worlds is infinite, some worlds being similar to this one <our own,> while other worlds are very different <from ours.> As has been shown, the number of the atoms is infinite and they are carried about to vast distances far away. Indeed, such <an infinite number of> atoms, of which a world is composed or out of which a world may be made, could not have been consumed and exhausted in the production either of one world or of a finite number of worlds—whether such worlds are similar to ours or different from it. Therefore, there is nothing to prevent there being an infinite number of worlds.

Sense Perception

There are patterns of shapes similar to those of solid bodies but quite different from any appearance we know on account of their fine-grained quality. Because it is not beyond the power of nature to make such subtly refined lengths of space within the all-encompassing <empty space;> nor to make such skillfully fine-tuned arrangements that can craft the hollow and smooth surfaces; nor to make outflows maintain the same <coordinate> positions on two dimensions, which they had analogously when they were in the solid bodies. And we call such patterns images. As their movement through space meets no countervailing resistance from bodies that could rebuff them, these images can complete any conceivable distance in an inconceivably short period of time. Indeed, the fact that motion has been resisted and the fact that this has not happened are other ways of saying, respectively, "slow speed" and "fast speed."

Time and the Speed of Moving Bodies

But, within time intervals which the mind is able to contemplate, it is not possible that a moving body can reach any significantly large number of places—this would indeed be inconceivable <as it would be tantamount to exceeding the speed of thought by means of. . .thinking.>

Nor can it ever be the case that, within perceptible time, a body can arrive here from anywhere in the unlimited void.

Yet it is also the case that a body is not really moving in its advance *from* the locus onto which we mentally project the perceived trajectory. The reason is this: we do not correct the moving body's velocity, which we compute in our minds, to take into account retarding influences <which have supervened;> and yet, forces with such a retarding impact have indeed been operating.

It is useful to keep firmly in mind this elementary proposition <of our system.> Nothing from the realm of appearances contradicts <the claim> that the image make use, so to speak, of an unsurpassedly fine-grained quality. Therefore, their velocities are also unsurpassed, since they have every path cut to their dimensions: the reason being that, not only are they infinite in number but, nothing or very little can collide with them effectively and arrest their movements. This is true even though it is also the case that a great—indeed, an infinite—number of them do actually have their movements arrested. <Because the total number is infinite, and infinity subtracted from infinity still leaves infinity.>

In addition, <nothing from the realm of appearances or visible phenomena contradicts the notion that> the production of images happens with speed equal with that of thought-event.

And the secretion of images <from bodies> is ongoing and continuous, even though this does not become evident from any reduction <in the size of the body> thanks to the counterbalancing replenishment which preserves the relative positions and order of the atoms in the solid object over a considerable period of time—although <this structural order> sometimes is thrown into a state of disarray.

The composite <images> in the circumambient space are acute-angled and <hence, sharply impinge on> the eye <to produce vision;> this is possible because vision cannot see through the plenum along the dimension of depth.

And there are ways too, in which such natures <i.e., the images> come into existence.

And nothing of all this is contradicted by sense perception, provided that one takes always into consideration the ways in which the clear and vivid stimuli and their harmoniously correlated affects some to us from outside <to form sense data inside us.>

And we must also accept that we see and form mental images of the shapes only if and insofar as something enters into us from outside. For the external objects could not be stamping their intrinsic natures of color and shape all over the air that lies between us and themselves; nor could they ever reach us by means of currents or rays that happened to be emanating from them. But they could very well reach us by means of certain patterns that enter into us coming straight from the objects and having the same colors and the same shapes as those objects. Such patterns engender vision or the illusory formation of mental images after the fact and they do so suitably and in accordance with the respective sizes.

This is the reason why the object itself is perceived as unitary and perduring in time. The images are able to do this because they preserve the characteristic corresponding affect of the external object as they carry this affect all the way from the object to produce an analogous impact. And this <characteristic affect of the object> originates in the pulsation of the atoms in the depth of the solid object.

And, whether we form the mental image by relying predominantly on thinking or sense perception; and whether the mental image has the shape or accidental properties of the object: such a mental image is, at any rate, one and the same since it is always created in accordance with <a process of> serial compacting of the left-over residue of the images.

Verificationist Theory of Error

Misrepresentation and error reside always in the beliefs which have been added onto what has been left over <from the images.> <There is, however, a simple test to apply in this case:> <The added beliefs are indifferent as to between> confirmation and disconfirmation.

Indeed, there can never be a recurrent <hence reliable> similarity between, on the one hand, mental images, what arises in sleep, or what is engendered from applications of the intellect or any other faculty of judgment; and, on the other hand, what are considered to be beings that exist truly and are true to speak of. Unless such things <i.e., the figments of imagination, etc.> existed and themselves impinged on us from outside!

Empiricist Epistemology

And it is imperative to be firmly in hold of this maxim too, so that we neither forfeit the judgments that are based on clear and vivid sense perceptions nor take erroneous judgments to be of equal certainty <as the ones based on vivid sense perception.> Indeed, this <acceptance of erroneous judgments> would throw everything into disarray.

Hearing

Hearing takes place when a certain kind of current is carried <all the way> from the person who speaks, makes a noise, causes some sound to be made by inflicting an impact, or in any way and at any time produces an auditory sensation.

This current disperses throughout the air; it is constituted of small masses of similar parts, which bear a certain affinity to one another and retain a mutual coordination of effects as well as a characteristic shared quality that stresses all the way back to objects from which the current originated. These masses of the current create the sense perception which characteristically corresponds to the object. If they fail to do so, they only make the external object visible <but not audible.>

Without such a mutual coordination of characteristic effects, which can be referred back <to the object that sent off the current> this sense perception of hearing could not be produced.

And one should think that the air itself is shaped by the emitted voice and by things of the same kind—because it is far from being the case that the air can ever be affected in this way by voice or sound—but it is rather like this: As soon as the blow takes place within us, when we send off a sound, this—we should understand—brings about a change in the trajectory of the small masses, which, in this way, come to form a breath-like current; it is this current that produces the auditory sensation in us.

The Sensation of Smell

And similarly with the sensation of smell: it should be understood that no such affect would ever be produced if it were not for certain masses which issue from the object. Such masses have a size that is congruent with the size of the object; the masses set our sense faculty in motion—some of them creating an upsetting and strange impression and others creating smooth and familiar impressions.

On the Nature of the Atom

We should also accept that the atoms do not present any of the apparent attributes of sensible objects, except for shape, weight, size, and every property which is, by natural necessity, conjoined with the property of shape. This is because every sensible attribute changes over time but the atoms do not change in any respect. Indeed, <the atoms must be immutable> if there is anything solid and indissoluble that remains and perdures when composites are dissolved; so that the changes are not from non-being and are not into non-being. Changes rather take place in accordance with the transpositions of the atoms.

It follows from this that the units that are transposed <to form composites> must necessarily be indestructible and cannot possibly have the same nature as the composite which is undergoing the change; they must rather have their own characteristic masses and configurations.

For the foundation of things must necessarily be such <i.e., indestructible.> Even with respect to the things which are directly changed by us, it is commonly accepted that the shape is inherent in the objects whereas the attributes do not inhere in the object which is undergoing a transformation. While the shape is still left <after the process of transformation has ended,> the attributes have now been lost from the object. The residues <from the process> must be able to account for the differences <in attributes> between the composites <involved in the whole process.> Indeed it is necessary that some residue be left from the process because nothing disappears by being transformed into non-being.

The Sizes of Atoms

On the other hand, one should not think that atoms can have each and every possible size; we need to assume this so as not to be contradicted by appearances. We should rather think that there are certain variations in atomic sizes. Because, if this principle is added, it will be easier to describe adequately the affects and sensations which clearly happen to us.

Indeed, to stipulate that every possible atomic size exists is not useful for accounting for the differences between attributes of objects. Moreover, <if an infinite number of atomic sizes existed,> certain sizes would also have to exist which would be visible to us. But there is no possibility of this ever happening; nor can we ever conceive how this could happen and how an atom could be visible.

The Number of Atoms in an Object

In addition, one should not think that, in a body that has clearly defined boundaries, an infinite number of masses can ever exist—no matter how infinitesimally small such masses may be.

So, we must deny that it is possible to continue to sub-divide into smaller pieces ad infinitum—this would indeed render all things ultimately impotent and compel us, in our efforts to take stock of the assemblages of units, to <assume that> certain beings <atoms> are squeezed and exhausted as if they were non-beings.

Moreover, we must also not accept that movements over progressively shorter distances can continue ad infinitum within clearly demarcated bodies <of finite size.>

There is really no way in which one could conceive how an infinite number of masses can exist within an object, no matter how small those masses may be: for how could such a magnitude still be demarcated and finite <if it contained an infinite number of masses?>

Because, even being infinitesimally small, the whole number of the masses would still have an <infinite> size. Indeed, no matter how small each size were, the whole size would still be infinite and impossible to demarcate.

Because, since what is bounded has a given, definite boundary—even if the edge is not visible in itself—it is impossible not to think of what is next to it as being of the same kind <i.e., bounded and with a marked boundary.> And, by taking incremental steps in both directions, one can arrive at the infinite—but simply by means of conceptualization or in thought.

On Whether Atoms Can be Traversed

As for the minimal part <i.e., the atom,> we must understand well that it is not like that which can be traversed; nor is it unlike that which can be traversed in every respect. It is rather that the minimum part has some attributes in common with the things that can be traversed over; but, unlike them, it does not contain any parts. But when, on account of the resemblances that present themselves, we come to believe that we can grab some part of <the atom> here on this side or that other part on the other side—it must needs be the case that the exact same thing falls into our possession.

A Thought Experiment

Assume that we view these minima the one next to the other, starting from the very first but without lingering in the same spot and, also, not as if we were repeating the exact same experience from one to the next, and without touching any parts by means of other parts; but rather <assume> taking measurements of magnitudes respectively by means of the attributes that are peculiar to each individual atom—the larger measuring more and the smaller fewer.

It should be understood that the minimum makes use of the same way of relating unique measuring unit to what is being measured.

It is obvious, indeed, that, on account of its small size, the minimum is different from what is perceived by the senses. But, still, it uses the same relationships <of measurement> by uniquely applying measuring unit to what is being measured.

Size of the Atom and Other. . .Loose Ends

And we have also predicated of the atom that it has a magnitude. In accordance with was said above <that, in atomic measurements, there is a unique commensurability between measuring unit and what is being measured> {each atom is self-measuring: on that basis, it is to be asserted that the atom has a size. Indeed, it would be impossible to apply any common measuring rod or unit to any atom because the atom has no parts.}

It is a small stretch, then, to apply this method of unique measurement to the atom.

We should accept that the minima are also the unadulterated edges or bounds <of objects> and can be of any length; so, the measuring process is ultimately on the basis of these elementary units, whether what is being measured is large or small. ***

. . .by means of rational theorizing about what are invisible things.

The resemblances between the atoms and those visible things which also do not admit of being traversed suffices to allow us to complete our account up to this point.

But it should be noted that it is impossible for such minima to be brought together and converge, even if they are in motion.

On Space

As for unbounded space, *** we should not predicate "above" or "below" of any parts of it in the sense of a highest or lowest point. {We can only refer to a relative, not to an absolute, orientation in space.} We can refer to what is over our heads relative to where we stand; but, were we to project this unto infinity by means of a line perpendicular to our heads, this projection would be lost from our vision as it was tending to infinity.

Also, consider this: If we were to draw the same imaginary line stretching to infinity underneath us, "below" and "above" would turn out to be one and the same. The reason is that it is impossible to conceive <infinite extension.> {Whereas, on the other hand, relative positions depend on our actual perceptual abilities.}

A Thought Experiment

Assume that there is an imaginary straight line stretching in one direction over our heads unto infinity; and also assume another line stretching underneath us and directed downwards. Assume now that something we carried were to pass through the feet and reach the heads of those above us countless times; and that something we carried downwards were to reach the heads of those below us <countless times.> Nevertheless, the two directions are conceived as being opposite—one upwards and one downwards—and extending unto infinity.

On the Velocities of the Atoms

It must also be the case that the atoms move with equal velocities when they move through empty space because nothing collides with them there to block and retard their motion. And the heavier things will not move any more quickly than the smaller and hollow ones whenever there is nothing to meet them in their paths. Likewise, the small things will not move more slowly than the large ones <through empty space> because <there>

they all have trajectories cut to their shapes <through which they can move smoothly> since nothing collides with them to block their motion.

And the upward motion is no different when it comes to velocity; and the same holds for sideways trajectories—which do indeed occur when the atoms bounce off from collisions, while, on the other hand, bodies follow downward trajectories of their own weights.

For as long as any <atom> maintains its velocity—which has been imparted to it either from an external source of by its own weight—to that extent it will continue with the same uniform velocity: and this is the same as the velocity with which thoughts are formed. This movement of the atom will continue until something collides with it and blocks its motion.

With respect to composites too, it ought to be said that, atoms having equal velocities <through empty space,> no atom moves more quickly than any other. And it should also be said that, when the atoms happen to come into place to form aggregates, they take the shortest possible time as they move continuously and without interruptions of their trajectories; otherwise, they could not converge toward one and the same spot.

Still, the truth is that atoms do collide and are blocked quite frequently—that is, to such an extent that the uninterrupted trajectories, which we perceive, are also made possible.

Moreover, the opinion that is held regarding invisible things—according to which the units of time perceived by the mind are continuous—is not true about such things. Indeed, only what is contemplated by the mind—and not what is accepted by common opinion and convention—is always true.

Composition of the Soul

Next, by taking our bearings from sense perception and from feelings—because the most certain conviction can be had in this way—we must take a comprehensive view of the fact that the soul is a body of exceedingly refined parts; and these parts are sown about throughout the entire aggregate <which is the person.> The soul is more closely related in its nature to breath than to anything else; and it also has an admixture of what-is-hot to some extent. So, it is akin to breath in certain respects and to what-is-hot in others. And there is also a part of the soul which is very different from the other two in terms of its fine-grained quality. The whole aggregate suffers the same affects as this <third part of the soul> does to a much greater extent than it is affected by the other two parts.

That this is the case is conclusively established by <inquiring into> the powers of the soul, its affects, its lithe mobility, the thought processes, and, in general, all those things, cessation of which entails death.

The Soul and Sensation

Moreover, we must maintain that the soul is responsible for sense perception more than anything else is.

But the soul would not have received this <power> if it were not somehow housed by the rest of the aggregate.

Interaction between Soul and Body

On the other hand, the rest of the aggregate also has become able to <have sense perception,> even though it is initially the soul that is solely responsible for, and productive of, <the ability to have sense perception.> <And this has come to be because> the rest of the aggregate has incidentally acquired this ability <of possessing sense perception> by having received it from the soul.

Nevertheless, <the rest of the aggregate> does not have all the abilities and properties, which the soul possesses. For this reason, when left by the soul, it does not have sense perception <anymore.> This is because it does not have this power of sense perception by itself but, rather, it acquired this ability by <incidentally> coming to exist simultaneously with the soul.

The soul, on the other hand, owns this power <of sense perception> in itself and has it already complete and consummate and fully actualized; and it imparts this power by means of <transmitting>

motion <to the body.> This is possible thanks to the <incidental> fact that the two—soul and body—come to share common boundaries; also thanks to their shared receptivity <i.e., natural ability to be affected by the same things.>

All this is consistent with what I had said previously.

On the Perdurance and Death of the Soul

This is the reason why the soul, insofar as it remains in existence within the body, will not lose its ability to have sense perception even if some other part of the body is lost: No matter which parts of the housing edifice are lost along with the body, and regardless as to whether only some part <of the body> or the whole of it is lost, insofar as the soul perdures it will still have sense perception {in the form of imagination perhaps.}

On the other hand, however, even if the whole aggregate were to remain, in part or even in its entirety, it would no longer have sense perception if and when the soul had been lost—and this is true regardless of how large or how small the magnitude of atoms that converge to constitute the soul is.

And, once the whole aggregate is dissolved, the soul scatters about like diffuse seeds and no longer has the same power; nor can the soul move anymore: hence, the soul can no longer have possession of its <erstwhile> power of sense perception.

A Thought Experiment

It is, indeed, impossible to conceive the faculty of sense perception as not existing <strictly> within this specific kind of coordinated apparatus; or as <once so existing> not making use of such motions <as become possible within the whole body-soul system.>

<On the other hand, however, one would have to conceive an absurdity if one were to think of the soul as still retaining sense perception> when the housing and encompassing edifice no longer is like the one within which the soul had those movements <which make sense perception possible.>

The Corporeality of the Soul

Moreover, one must also make sure to grasp this: We commonly apply the term "incorporeal" to that which can be thought of as existing by itself. But there is no way one can conceive of something incorporeal that exists simply by itself—unless it be empty space.

But empty space cannot make anything happen and cannot itself be affected by anything in any way; it only makes available to bodies movement through itself.

So, those who say that the soul is incorporeal are speaking in vain.

Because, if the soul were incorporeal, it could not make anything happen and it could not be affected in any way. And yet it is perfectly clear that both of these <i.e., acting and being acted upon> clearly happen to the soul.

Were one to refer all the confusions regarding the soul to <what has been said about> affects and sense perception, keeping in mind also what was said in the beginning <of this letter,> one would be able to take a complete survey of all that is contained in our theoretical formulas and, on that basis, to figure out any <remaining> details with precision.

Permanent and Incidential Properties of Bodies

And when it comes to the shapes and colors and sizes and weights and all those other attributes which are predicated of a body—whether these be attributes that happen to be inhering to all bodies or only to those which are visible and known to us by virtue of sense perception: we should not think that such natures <i.e., shapes and colors and sizes and weights> exist independently by themselves

—because it is not possible to conceive this being the case; we should not think—<going to the other extreme>—that they do not exist at all; we should not think of them as some other kind of natural entity which happens to exist in addition and as attached to the body; and we should not think of them as being portions of the body.

Rather we should think that the entire body, taken as a whole and considered generally, has its permanent nature from all these properties; but not as if <the whole body> were concocted from all these thrown together—as is the case when a large aggregate comes to be constituted either by primary masses which are brought together or when it assumes successive integral identities as its constituent masses diminish: but <we should think of the body as being made of properties> only in the sense that the whole body has its own characteristic nature constituted of all these properties. And all these <properties> have each its own characteristic and unique way of striking <the sensory faculties> and of being perceived and understood, provided that the overall assemblage is still intact and goes along with the <properties> and is in no way torn apart from them.

So, the meaning of the word body refers to the sum of all the properties which are predicated of a body and which a body has obtained.

It often happens, however, that many accidents befall a body *** and such are to be classed neither among the <material but> invisible things nor among the <presumed> incorporeal things.

So, for the most part, whenever we make use of this term <i.e., "accident",> we should make it clear that the incidental properties, which have befallen the body, do not have the same nature as the whole does—which, nature, we predicate of the body when and insofar as we conceive it as an assemblage <of perduring properties;> and also, we should make it clear that the incidental properties are not always accompanied by the permanent properties of the body: but it is, indeed, <only> these permanent properties of a body that make it possible to conceive of the meaning of the word "body."

We can identify incidental properties only insofar as they impinge on <our sensory faculties> and when, at the same time, the whole body is <perceived as being> in conjunction with the incidental properties. ***

The incidental properties can be conceived for what they are—each one separately—only for the duration over which each one happens to befall the body. Because, indeed, such incidental properties are not in permanent conjunction with <the body.>

On the other hand, we should not reject such incidental properties insofar as we have very clear perception of them as existent—we should not reject them simply because they do not have the same nature with that which they happen to befall or because they do not remain <for long> in conjunction with the permanent properties of bodies.

Nor should we, going to the other extreme, take the incidental properties as existing by themselves and independently—at any rate, this is indeed inconceivable anyway both in the case of incidental properties as well as in the case of properties which have been permanent <but are not anymore.>

We should rather take our bearings from what clearly appears to be the case: thus, we should take incidental properties to be merely incidental properties of their respective bodies, which are not in permanent conjunction with the body and are not members of an ordered natural class of their own.

Generally, incidental properties are to be understood in whatever way our sense perception makes their qualities register.

Time

One must also take special care to understand the following: we must inquire after the nature of time in the same way we do about the rest—i.e., all those things, which we seek to understand by taking stock of our subjective experiences when we refer everything to what visibly impinges on us from outside. We should rather try to grasp the meaning of time by drawing on what is very clear to us {i.e., by means of direct intuition}: We do this when we declare that a "short period of time" or a "long period of time" has elapsed by means of a built-in affinity <to time> which we have in us.

Let us reflect further on how exactly we can bring this about:

We should not alter the accepted meanings of common idiomatic expressions <about time> presuming to improve upon them; we should rather utilize the idiomatic expressions which are already in existence.

Nor should we predicate of time anything else—claiming, as it were, that time has the same nature with this or that particular quality—and this is exactly what some people are wont to do.

But we should rather take special care to consider time in terms of that peculiar quality, with which we always conjoin time <in our intuitions about time;> also in terms of that peculiar quality of time, which we use in order to measure time.

And we do not need a demonstration for this: we rather need to reflect. It is the case that we always associate time with days and nights and the parts of these; and similarly with feelings and with the absences of affects, and also with motion and rest—always conceiving of all these as having the same unique and specific property, according to which we define time.

Worlds

Returning to what was said previously, we must understand that each world, as well as every bounded and sufficiently compacted totality that is similar and of the same kind as the one we see, has been born out of the unlimited: this is true of all of them—larger and small alike. They have all been winnowed and separated into distinct regions according to the varying diameters of their revolutions. And they are all to be dissolved again—some more quickly and others more slowly and through the operation of all kinds of factors.

Moreover, we should not think that all the worlds have, of natural necessity as it were, one and the same configuration. *** No one could prove that, in such and such a world, the seeds were not <in fact> included, of which the animals and the plants and the rest that are seen <here among us> have come to be. And, for any kind of world, no one could prove that <those seeds> could not have been possibly included.

On the Original Condition of Human Nature

One must assume that human nature has learned out of necessity and directly from circumstances. And one must assume that reason attended with precision to, and discovered more about, what necessity had vouchsafed—<nature making knowledge available initially only> in a chaotic manner. This happened more quickly with respect to certain things than to others. And, in certain periods, <progress was more rapid> ***, but in others <progress was slower.>

Naming and the Meaning of Words

The names of things were not posited at the beginning as a matter of convention; rather, it was the case that, <human nature being what it is,> human beings were affected by the same affects uniquely within each human community; and receiving unique impressions <from their surroundings,> human beings would emit breath in their specific ways, triggered by their corresponding feelings and impressions: the result was the difference <in language> which we find among different human communities.

It was only later that each community posited <and fixed> by convention the specific <references of words> in order to render meanings less ambiguous and more succinct for the purposes of communication. And, as those who became jointly aware of new things had to introduce those <novelties,> which had not been encompassed by their common language up to that point, they were compelled to also make available new word-units in order to be able to refer to them <publicly.> At least this is the case for those who introduced new words deliberately; for the most part they applied the aforementioned method in setting the conventional public meanings of the new words for the purpose of communication.

The Celestial Phenomena

When it comes to meteorological matters—i.e., the movements, revolutions, eclipses, risings, and settings, and everything related to these—it should not be thought that these happen because someone is functioning as an operator <of this whole celestial structure;> or because someone sets to order and commands. Especially this cannot be the case if this someone is, additionally, supposed to have every blessed joy and to be indestructible:

Because being a busy-body and functioning as a care-taker—and, also, beings presumably given to bouts of wrath and tending to bestow favors—all these things are incompatible with a state of blissful blessedness but happen rather to one who is ill or in fear and in need of those nearby.

Nor, again, would those celestial ignitions of twisted fire assume such motions by their own volition if they had been already in a blessed state.

We should rather see to it that we maintain a sense of solemnity in every respect when we apply words to refer to such concepts: we need to do this in order to prevent contrary <and debased> notions from arising when it comes to the things that <truly merit> solemn treatment. Were to fail in this, the inconsistency <which would result> would engender the greatest turmoil in human souls.

To this effect, we must embrace the opinion that those orderly and regular revolutions <of the celestial bodies> take place out of natural necessity and in accordance with the rotations, which those bodies received from the very beginning, when <this particular> world came into existence.

Science Ought to Replace Superstition

We must also accept that it is the work of natural science to investigate with precision the factors which are responsible for the principal meteorological phenomena. It is blessed joy that really falls to the share of one who studies these phenomena—one who knows what those celestial natures consist in and everything that conduces to precision in the knowledge of such matters.

The Study of Natural Science

Moreover, <we should understand that> "for the most part" and "it might be the case that it is otherwise" do not apply to the study of nature. It is rather that all those factors, which introduce disturbances and make qualifying distinctions necessary, do not exist among indestructible and blessed natures.

What falls to the share of one who merely charts the record of settings and risings and revolutions and eclipses and all their kindred phenomena—knowledge obtained in this way <simply by recording charts> does not in any way redound to a blessed state. Those who know only such things—no matter how expert their specific <narrow> knowledge is—are still ignorant as to what the natures of the celestial bodies and the fundamental meteorological processes are; they still live in fear and as if they had no knowledge at all. Possibly, such students have even worse fears <than those who are completely ignorant> insofar as, in their case, the dazzling wonderment that is aroused by the attentive study of celestial bodies is unable to find a satisfying resolution—a solution that is consistent with the governing logic of the fundamental meteorological processes. For this reason, no matter how many additional processes we come up with in order to explain appearances regarding revolutions and settings and risings and eclipses and such matters—as usually happens with specific applied inquiries—we should still never dismiss the deeper study <of fundamental processes,> nor should we ever believe that such studies have failed to attain precision. It is rather this latter kind of study that conduces to our obtaining a state of imperturbable tranquility and joyful blessedness.

Notes on Method

So, we should take an all-around survey of the many ways in which the same phenomenon <is observed to> take place. And we should do this by making explanatory inferences about the meteorological processes and everything that is not evident to the senses; and we should have deserved contempt for those who do not know that certain phenomena are singular occurrences or that we should always consider the distances involved; and should also disdain those who are ignorant as to what matters we should not bother about.

But if in addition to knowing a particular kind of way, in which something might chance to happen, we also know that it might happen in many other ways, then we will be as free of anguish as if it were actually the case that the phenomenon can happen only in the way we know.

Human Fears and How to Assuage Them

In addition to all the above, one must generally understand that the greatest distress befalls the human soul because of the belief that those celestial bodies have wishes and undertake actions and are responsible <for certain events> even though they are blessed and indestructible beings. Yet the former attributes are in contradiction with the latter <i.e., having wishes and undertaking actions are incompatible with being blessed and indestructible.>

And fears also arise from the perpetual expectation that some eternal and formidable harm <might befall one at any time> and from suspecting <that this is about to happen> in accordance with the popular fairy tales.

And anguish also arises because of the fearful anticipation of the absence of sense perception, which is entailed by death— as if death had anything to do with human beings—{i.e., when death happens, the human being is not in existence anymore}.

And anguish also arises because these <anticipatory> sufferings are incurred not through reasoned opinion but by means of an irrational representation <of claims about an afterlife.> Because of this, i.e., because they do not draw proper boundaries around the possible range of wondrous things by using their reason, people suffer an equal—or, actually, a much more intensified—state of mental distress than if they had reasoned about what is logically possible.

Imperturbability, on the other hand, consists in having been released from all this and in retaining constant memory of all, and especially of the principal, points <of my philosophic system.> From which it follows that one must always pay attention to the emotions and to the data of sense perception—accordingly taking into consideration whether they are common to all humankind or unique and private; moreover, one should always pay attention singly to each present occurrence and strictly following the clear and vivid evidence according to criteria <which are supplied by my system.>

And, if we pay attention to all these points, we shall be able to rightly explain and account for the forces which are responsible for all human fears and distress and, hence, rid ourselves of those fears.

<An example of this is the case of> meteorological phenomena and such occurrences as are always bound to happen and which mightily frighten the common run of humanity. We, on the other hand, are able to explain them and provide an account for the forces which are responsible for such phenomena.

Conclusion

All the above are the principal points <of the system> concerning the nature of the universe and are here offered as a comprehensive summary for your benefit, Herodotus.

So, if it is possible for someone to get a grip on the points made in this summary and retain them with minute precision, I believe that such a person would be able to have unsurpassable strength <of soul> compared to others—and this one can do even if he does not step into the precise discourses <which I have also composed> on various details.

Because, among other things, he will be able to clarify, by his own efforts, many a specific point that we have addressed with precision in our <detailed> discourses; and etching all this into memory will surely be a constant source of assistance.

Moreover, the teachings in the present summary are such that, even for those who have already attended to the specific and precise discourses sufficiently well, or even for those who have worked out all the details and done so to completion of their studies—even they could make out most of the points of the system about the nature of the universe <by memorizing the present summary.>

Those, on the other hand, who have not reached consummate expertise in our complete discourses, may still, by following the method that does not require direct lecturing, make it possible for themselves, as fast as thought races, to attain tranquility.

EPICURUS,

LETTER TO PYTHOCLES

{Diogenes Laertius X.83–116}

FROM Epicurus to Pythocles: Greetings.

Introduction

Cleon has brought me a letter from you, in which you show your-self abidingly stalwart in your good will toward me—hence, deserving the good care <I have bestowed on you;> <in the same letter,> you attempt, rather convincingly, to recollect the thoughts that conduce to a blessed life; and you express the need you have for me to send you a brief and concise meditation on meteorological phenomena, so that you can memorize <the main points> with facility.

Because, indeed, what I have written on this subject elsewhere is difficult to retain in memory even though, as you say, you have those <teachings> constantly in hand.

As for my part, I accepted your request gladly and was seized by sweet hope.

Having, therefore, composed all that follows, I am able to fulfill your request. These reflections are going to be useful to many more <besides you>—especially to those who have only recently savored the genuine philosophy of nature; and also to those who happen to be tangled up in some pursuit more profound than the study of the compendious discourses.

So, receive the present document with firm and secure grip and, retaining them acutely in memory, mull over <its contents> along with the rest <included in the letter> I sent to Herodotus in a Lesser Summary.

The Purpose of Meteorological Studies

First and foremost, one should not think that there is any other purpose to the study of celestial phenomena—whether studied in conjunction with other teachings or independently—besides the production of imperturbable tranquility and unshakable conviction—as is true of the rest <of natural philosophy.>

Appropriate Method

We should not try to attain what is impossible—trying to force theories <to fit ulterior purposes;> nor should we aim at having a theory that is the same in all respects with the teachings on the other problems of natural philosophy or with the discourses on how to live one's life well and properly—like, for instance, the teaching, according to which all that exists consists solely of bodies and the intangible <i.e., empty space,> or that the fundamental constitutive elements of all bodies are uncuttable atoms, or that <only such things are to be admitted as> are consistent with visible appearances.

There is no single teaching on the celestial phenomena: rather, there are multiple ways by means of which such phenomena are generated and there is a plurality of theorizing accounts, by means of which the natures of celestial phenomena are revealed to be consistent with <phenomena directly known through> sense perception.

For we should not discourse on natural phenomena in accordance with vacuous dogma and as if we were after law-like regularities; rather we should discourse them strictly as the phenomena themselves dictate.

Because our lives have no need of irrational babble and hollow beliefs—enough of this we have heard already!—but of <specifics about> how we can live without disturbance.

Everything <in nature> happens without much ado and all phenomena can be reconciled with multiple <plausible> theoretical accounts—provided that all those accounts are consistent with visible appearances; this can be done insofar as one allows only for what can be said with plausibility <and for nothing more>—this is what one should always do in every instance anyway.

But, when one allows for some accounts and rejects others which are equally consistent with appearances, it is obvious that such an observer has taken leave of each and every natural-theoretical accounts and has lapsed into mythology.

Certain occurrences that are similar to what transpires up high above are indeed presented by sensible phenomena which are accessible to us—at least, they are deemed to be happening so; but, generally speaking, the meteorological phenomena <are not accessible for us to observe directly.> For they can occur in any one of many ways <hence, in more ways than we are familiar with from direct experience.>

Yet, the impressions made on us by each meteorological phenomenon ought to be documented assiduously and other phenomena, which occur in conjunction with celestial phenomena, ought to be <recorded and> classified—provided that there is no contrary evidence from other phenomena which take place regularly and are brought to completion <within the realm of our direct experience.>

A World (Cosmos)

A world is a region of the sky which is demarcated all around and set off <from adjacent regions,> and which contains stars and an earth and all the natural phenomena, and which is cut off from the boundless <empty space> and terminates <in a boundary> which is either revolving or stationary and has a spherical, solid-triangular, or any other shape.

Each and every possibility is admissible. Because none of the phenomena, which are visible to us in this our world, presents evidence to the contrary since it is impossible <for us here> to perceive the boundary <of our world.>

Number of Worlds

And it must be understood that an unlimited number of such worlds exists; and also that such a world can come into existence both within an already existent world as well as in any one of the regions between any two worlds—which is the so-called interval between worlds—a place that is, for the most part, empty space and is not, as some contend, a grand vacant area.

<This formation of a world happens when> certain seeds of the appropriate type flow from one world or region-between-worlds—or even from more than one—and, before too long, begin to form annexes and articulated conjunctions and "migrations" to other places. This can happen by mere chance. And superadded influxes from of the appropriate types <of atoms> <may indeed continue by chance> until the whole is consummated and, hence, becomes able to abide and stay put—provided, of course, that the foundation, which had been laid previously, is capable of admitting and supporting the incoming matter.

Because it is not plausible that this can happen solely by means of assemblages or vortices <of atoms> in empty space whose size waxes in accordance with natural necessity until another world collides with it—this is what some of the so-called specialists of natural studies have claimed! This theory is indeed inconsistent with the phenomena that are visible to us.

Celestial Bodies

The sun and the moon and the other shining celestial bodies are not generated in and by themselves, to be included along with the rest of the universe subsequently, but are formed and increase in size right away by means of annexations <of material chunks> and vortex-like rotations of certain fine-grained masses—which are fire-like, breath-like, or of both types.

Indeed, this is what sense perception attests to.

And the <relative> sizes of the sun and the moon and the rest of the shining celestial bodies are such as they appear to be. Taken by itself, the size of a celestial body can <logically> be either greater, smaller than, or exactly the same as it appears to us. Because, indeed, in our own directly accessible experience, burning fires, seen from a distance, are regarded by our senses in the same way <i.e., in accordance with the above three logically possible relations of apparent to true size.> And every dispute and objection about this can be handled easily and can be surmounted if one only pays attention to the clear and vivid impressions afforded us by our senses. We have shown this in our writings on Nature.

Risings and Settings

It is possible that the risings and settings of the sun, the moon, and the rest of the celestial bodies happen accordingly as kindling and extinguishing <of their fires> take place—and this, again, may be happening when the surrounding conditions are such that the aforementioned <risings and settings> can be completed. For there is nothing among the phenomena we know from observation, which testifies against this <possibility.> Or, it could be that the risings and settings are actualized accordingly as the <celestial bodies> appear, time and again, to be suspended over the earth. Because, to repeat, nothing among the phenomena we observe testifies against this possibility.

And it is not impossible that the motions of the celestial bodies happen because of the vortex-like rotation of the sky. Or, if the sky is stationary, because the celestial bodies themselves are moving in a vortex-like rotational fashion in accordance with the natural necessity that originated in the generation of the universe when the first rising took place. ***

...because of a most intense heating engendered by some kind of perennial blowing of the cosmic blaze as it moves from one region to the adjacent one.

Higher and Lower Positions on the Firmament

The higher and lower positions of the sun and moon on the firmament might be possibly the result of the fact that the sky slants in a rather oblique angle—this obliqueness being forcefully implanted on the sky by the different seasons. Similarly, <all this could be produced> because the air rushes to flow out in an opposite direction. Or because flammable material of the suitable kind is constantly ablaze. Or even because there is insufficient material. Or because from the very beginning there was such a vortex-like rotation imparted to those stars so that they were, right away, made to move in a spiral-like fashion.

All these explanations and other related to them are not at variance with any of the clear and vivid impressions which we receive from sense perception, if one judges whether a theoretical account is possible by referring to what is consistent with the visible appearances and without paying heed to or being frightened of the slavish artifices of the star specialists.

Waxing and Waning of the Moon

The waning of the moon, as well as its subsequent waxing, could be happening because of the manner in which this body rotates or, likewise, because of the ways in which the air forms and changes shapes. Or, again, it could be due to accretions or, in general, it could be happening for any reason and in any way in which similar phenomena that are directly accessible to us take place.

Warning about Methodology

{As a general rule,} one should not disapprove of any explanatory account because one has become partial to one single explanatory account. When this happens, one fails to discern what is feasible and what is not feasible by human standards and, consequently, one is reduced to wishing for what is even impossible to comprehend.

The Moon's Light

Moreover, it is possible both that the moon has its light in and by itself and that it receives its light from the sun.

Because, in our accessible experience, many objects are observed which have light by themselves and many others are also observed which receive light from others.

And, indeed, there is nothing that prevents meteorological phenomena <from working exactly as observable and visible phenomena do.>

Methodological Comment

As a general rule, one should always remember that the best approach is the one that relies on multiple <plausible> accounts. Additionally, one should always take a synoptic view of the assumptions that are generated and of the reasons that are given by the various accounts. And one should not attach disproportionate importance to inconsistencies or become trapped in blind alleys. These <methodological errors> impel, one way or another, to single-factor explanations.

The Supposed Face on the Moon

The apparent impression of a face on the moon could have been produced either because of transformations of the compositions of lunar parts or because of accretions <of new parts;> or, generally, in accordance with any way that is to be deemed consistent with the phenomena that are visible to us.

The Proper Method in Relation to the Ultimate Purpose of Studies

When it comes generally to all the celestial phenomena, one should never discard the investigative method <described above.> Because, if one were to start fighting against the testimony of clear and vivid sense perception, one would become unable to partake of genuine imperturbability ever again.

Eclipses of the Sun and Moon

Eclipses of the sun and moon could be happening because the fire is periodically extinguished—as is observed to happen in our own accessible experience. Or, eclipses could be happening because other bodies—earth, sky, or any such bodies—happen to be blocking <the sun or moon.>

It is imperative that we consider more than one explanatory account considering that the processes <involved in these phenomena> are naturally similar <to certain visible phenomena, with which we are familiar from experience. Also, we should bear in mind that it is not impossible that more than one explanatory accounts apply jointly.

Regular Motions of the Celestial Bodies and the Divine

In addition, we should understand the regular periodicity of <the motions of> the celestial bodies to be similar to certain phenomena which happen to be observed in ordinary experience. And, in no respect whatsoever should the divine nature be brought in to bear on such matters; the divine should rather be considered as being aloof from such processes and in a state of complete and blissful blessedness.

Because, if this rule is not observed, the entire inquiry into celestial phenomena will be reduced to futility—as has already happened to some who have failed to touch upon any plausible account and, having tumbled precipitously into vain efforts, think that everything happens in one and only one way. Having expelled all the other plausible accounts of celestial phenomena, and having reduced themselves to unaccountable obscurity, they are unable to obtain a synoptic view that would allow them to study celestial phenomena by means of observable signs.

Night and Day

The spans of days and nights vary because both the sun moves quickly over the earth and also because, at other times, the sun moves slowly *** as is observed in our accessible experience, consistently with which we should theorize about celestial phenomena.

But those who accept any one reason <as sufficient for an explanatory account> are waging battle against the appearances and have fallen off the path of empirically based theorizing that is accessible to human beings.

The Weather

Changes in the weather and in the signs by which we recognize and forecast such changes, may depend on convergences of conditions which are specific to seasons, as is obvious to us in the case of <the stages in the lives of> animals. Such changes may also happen because of modifications in the consistency, and other alterations, of the air.

For both the aforementioned are not inconsistent with the visible phenomena.

But it is not possible to obtain a complete picture as to which specific processes are responsible for each <weather event.>

Clouds and Rain

It is possible that clouds are generated by and composed of compressed layers of air or of mutual entwinings of atoms that are suitable for producing this outcome. It is also possible that clouds are created as a result of currents gathering together—such currents rising either from the earth or water.

And it is not impossible that the compositions <which we see as clouds> are produced in many other ways in addition <to what was mentioned above.>

The rain that follows the formation of clouds may be produced when these clouds undergo compression or certain other transformations.

Additionally, <it is possible that rain is produced> when winds, issuing from suitably situated locations, descend after they have been moving about throughout the air. And more powerful showers are produced by certain assemblages which are suitable for bringing about such downpours.

Thunder and Lightning

Similarly, lightning may be generated in multiple ways. One way is this: Due to friction or collision between clouds, the configuration <of atoms,> which produce fire, slide outward and produce the lightning.

It can also happen by means of shooting of sparks outwards from the clouds, so that a conflagration results; this happens when winds <buffet the clouds.> It can also happen by means of squeezing—when the clouds are squashed either by other clouds or by winds. And it can also be happening because the light, which is scattered about by the stars, is caught and encompassed by the clouds and, later, gets carried along within the moving clouds until it escapes through the clouds. Or, it may be happening because the most fine-grained light is filtered through the clouds and, as it moves, <it generates lightning.> And it may be happening due to the fact that the wind itself catches fire, which can happen because of the relative movement and extreme compression of <the wind that is caught by the clouds.>

And it may be happening when clouds are scattered by winds with the result that the atoms which produce fire escape from the clouds and form the visible appearance of lightning.

It will be easy to comprehend how such phenomena, which happen always in one of several definite ways, and phenomena similar to them, can take place.

Now, the reason why the lightning occurs before the thunder is this: Insofar as the arrangement of clouds is such <as was described above,> the configuration of atoms which produces fire is pushed out of the clouds simultaneously as the wind strikes the cloud; subsequently, the wind is caught up by the clouds and creates the characteristic booming sound of thunder.

Even if the two <lightning and thunder> occur simultaneously, it is the lightning that moves much faster relative to us whereas the <sound of the> thunder lags behind.

<As is well known,> this also happens when certain objects are observed from a distance to be striking other objects.

It is possible that the thunderbolt is generated when many wind currents assemble together in one place and when the extreme compression makes them catch fire. It is possible also that the thunderbolt is generated when one part of the cloud is fractured and collapses with a force that increases progressively as the cloud-part is falling toward lower layers of air—the fracture of the cloud happening, in the first place, because the adjacent places are denser due to a piling up of clouds. It is also possible that the thunderbolt happens because the fire is caught up and subsequently escapes by means of a process similar to the one that produces thunder: as more and more fire comes to be contained within the cloud and as the cloud is smitten by the winds more and more forcefully, the fire <becomes engorged and> ruptures the cloud; this happens because the cloud itself can no longer expand into the adjacent region on account of the fact that more and more clouds have been piling up around it.

It is indeed possible that the thunderbolt may be generated in any one of many more ways.

Only make sure that you stay away from myths! The way to do this is by making inferences about what cannot be seen on the basis of observations and by taking stock meticulously of what is accessible through observation.

Whirlwinds and Tornadoes

It is possible that whirlwinds are generated when a cloud settles down as it descends, shaped like a pillar, toward the lower places and because it has been forced by the wind that had been confined within the cloud; as it descends, the cloud is made to gyrate because of the exertion of force from the wind outside.

Or whirlwinds may chance to happen when wind has been set into a circular motion due to the fact that some layer of fine air has accumulated and is now pressing from above.

And, whirlwinds may be produced also when a mighty onrush of many wind currents happens to take place; in that case, a whirlwind will form if it is also the case that too much air has piled up around the rushing wind currents and prevents them from flowing sidewise.

When the whirlwind settles down on the earth, a tornado is generated; if on sea, a waterspout is formed.

Earthquakes

It is possible that earthquakes are generated because wind has been confined within the earth; also because small masses of earth, which are situated adjacent to each other, move constantly—which produces the characteristic vibration of the ground.

This wind is either brought into the earth from outside or it falls to the ground and enters into cavernous regions and is then blown inside to form the <aforementioned> masses of confined air.

It is also possible that earthquakes take place as a result of the transmission of the motion which is generated when masses of ground fall down and <other masses> reciprocate—something that happens when the falling masses meet more densely compacted areas.

And it is possible that these movements of the earth are generated in any one of many more ways. ***

<Volcanoes>

Occasionally it so happens that winds become confined within the earth: this occurs when something extraneous and of a kind different <from the nature of the material inside the earth> keeps slipping inside little by little; and also when abundant water has been collected. Other instances of the generation of such winds take place when a small number of wind currents fall into hollow regions and the <resultant> motion is transmitted subsequently.

Hail

Hail is formed due to a most forceful condensation, which takes place when certain wind-like currents happen to gather from all around and, subsequently, divide into several parts. Also, <hail can be produced> because of a less violent condensation of certain water-like particles: This happens when there is simultaneous confluent current, which enables the water-like particles to bond—in this way, they form either part by part or en masse.

It is not impossible that the spherical shape <of the hail> is generated by the melting away of the edges on all sides and because, as it is said, their composition is such that all the particles—whether water-made or breath-like—are arranged next to each other in an even and regular fashion.

Snow

It is possible that snow is formed when fine-grained <particles of> water flow out from clouds. The particles assume the shapes of <cloud> pores through which they pass. All this happens because, at the same time, clouds, which are suitable for this process, happen to be crushed by the winds with extreme force.

Subsequently, the snow globules receive solidification in the course of their downward movement when it so happens that the regions below the clouds are very cold.

Snow may also happen to form because of the solidification <of water> within the clouds: When such clouds have an even distribution of rarefied areas within them, such an outflow may be produced if water-formed clouds happen to be abutting and if they are then squeezed by rubbing against each other.

Such clouds make hail whenever they happen to form something like a composite—which happens mostly in the spring.

Snow may also be produced because of the friction between clouds which have already obtained a state of solidification. It is easy to shed snow which has accumulated in this way because of the vibration <resulting from the friction between the clouds.>

And it is possible that snow may be produced in many other ways too.

Dew

Dew is produced when particles which produce this kind of moisture converge. This happens because the particles are being carried either from damp areas or from places that have water in them—it is in the latter that dew is actualized most often. Subsequently, the particles converge to one spot and form a humid mass before they are carried back again to the lower regions—quite in a similar way to the one in which such phenomena are seen <to be actualized in our directly accessible experience.>

<And frost is produced in a similar way:> it is produced when dewy masses somehow obtain a solidified state because some cold air mass had happened to be surrounding them.

Ice

Ice is produced when two things happen in conjunction: The rounded configuration is squeezed out of the water mass; and, at the same time, the scalene- and acute-triangular particles, which are in the water, happen to converge. This all happens also because of the forceful inward thrust of such particles which, issuing from outside and entering in, tend to prepare a solidified state for the water mass by crushing a certain percentage of the rounded particles.

Rainbow

The rainbow is generated when the sun shines on air masses that are made of water. Or, the rainbow is produced by a peculiar admixture of light and air, which is able to produce the characteristic qualities of the colors—either all or any one of them.

If and when it so happens that light is reflected off, the adjacent masses of air receive a tincture of color like the one we are wont to see when the <reflected light> is received <by the adjacent masses.>

The perceptible appearance of an even circumference around the rainbow is due to the fact that vision sees equal lengths in all directions; or because the particles in the air come into mutual convergences <so that they become equally distributed in all directions;> or because, issuing from the sun as they do, the particles in the clouds impart <on the eyes> a sort of roundedness.

The Halo of the Moon

The halo around the moon is generated when air is carried toward the moon from other places; or when the currents which emanate from the moon itself in an even fashion are held back but only so much as is sufficient for forming a circular cloud-like formation, which is as rarefied as it can possibly be; or when the moon holds back the air around it in a symmetrical fashion in every direction so as to establish a thickly constituted, rotating formation.

All this can happen when, in certain places, a current of air rushes in violently from outside; or when heating works to produce this effect by taking up space so as to create pores that are fitting for this purpose.

Comets

Comets are generated when, under appropriate conditions which happen by chance, flames gather and are nourished together in one place; this can happen in certain regions and over certain periods of time. Comets may also be generated when, throughout the regular rotations of the sky above us, certain specific and suitable movements <make comets form or descend on us.> {Or because the comets themselves obtain impetus at certain times and as a result of random circumstances, so that they are able to enter into the regions near us and become visible. And their disappearance from our field of vision happens for the opposite reasons.}

Fixed Stars

Certain stars rotate fixed in one place. This happens to be the case not only, as some contend, because that one region of the universe <where fixed stars can be seen> is the one around which the rest revolves, but because <such stars> are enclosed all around by a circular vortex of air, which hinders those stars as it does not allow them to wander around as the other stars are able to do; or because there is no fitting matter on which they can "feed" in the adjacent regions while such matter exists only in the place where they are seen to be situated.

And this phenomenon can come to pass in many other ways besides the ones mentioned above. <One is at liberty to provide any suitable explanatory account> provided that one finds it possible to reconcile this account with the visible appearances <which are accessible to us from direct experience.>

Planets

Certain stars wander about—if it is indeed the case that they move in this way—and others move in a regular fashion. It may well be the case that all stars were moving in the circle in the beginning <of our world> and were subsequently constrained in such a way that some stayed within the trajectory of the original vortex, which was regular, while others were disturbed into some other vortex-like formation, which had irregularities.

It is also possible that these stars are carried into certain regions, within which the expanses of air are distributed evenly and in regular formations: so, these air formations goad all <the planets> even and in the same directions and fuel them regularly.

But, in other regions, it is possible that there are irregularities due to the uneven distribution of regions <of air expanses,> and this is the reason for the derogation from the standard path of orbiting, which we observe.

Note on Method

At any rate, to give an account that attributes all these phenomena to a single reason, whereas the phenomena we observe are screaming that multiple causes are at work, would be maniacal and inconsistent with our duty. This is indeed what certain fanatics practice in their vain astrology when they vacuously assign presumed reasons for the occurrences of astral processes. Those fanatics are at their worst especially when they do not even see fit to release the divine nature in the slightest from menial operations <in the supervision and guiding of planetary motions.>

Apparent Discrepancies in the Movements of Stars

Certain stars appear to have been left behind by the others: this may happen either because they move around in the same orbit but more slowly than the rest, or because they are moving in the opposite direction and on the same orbit <relative to the rest,> so they are held back; or, again, because some stars might be moving through fewer, and some through more, regions even though they all move on the same orbit.

But to make unqualified averments about such phenomena is the wonted habit of those who wish to woo the masses with tales about wonders and freaks.

Falling Stars

The so-called falling stars might be generated, in part, because clouds rub against each other so that fire flows out, so that a conflagration is triggered—similarly to what we said about lightning above.

Also, falling stars may be produced when particles which can create fire converge and, because of their mutual affinities, come together to precipitate this outcome. Moreover, falling stars may also be produced because of the movement which takes place in the direction of the original thrust that was imparted by the original convergence. Falling stars may also be produced because of the accumulation of wind which results in certain dense and foggy formations; these formations are set ablaze because of the confinement, thus causing a subsequent explosion of their contents. Such conflagrations cover expanses of space, whose length depends on the impetus of the initial explosion.

And there are other ways which may bring about such outcomes. These explanatory accounts are free from the taint of superstition.

Weather Signs

The predictive signs, which happen to certain animals, are a matter of mere coincidence. Because it is certainly not the case that the animals supply some necessitating force which compels winter to set in; nor is it the case that some divine being is seated to observe the egresses of such animals <from their places of hibernation> and subsequently arrange that the predictive signs are proven true.

Because, indeed, such moronic behavior could not even afflict any chance animal—if the animal happened to be even slightly gifted—let alone one who possesses blessed and consummate bliss.

Exhortation and Conclusion

Pythocles, commit all that you find in this letter to memory. By so doing, you will be able to stay clear from mythological superstition and, by taking a synoptic view of all that can be known, you will be able to account for the various phenomena which are similar in kind to the ones <covered in the present letter.>

Above all, devote yourself unreservedly to the task of theorizing about origins and principles and about the boundless void and related concepts; also keep reflecting on the criteria, on the basis of which judgments are to be made, and on the effects of the emotions and, in general, on all those reasons, on account of which we find ourselves compelled to ruminate on such things.

Once all these factors have been taken in according to a properly synoptic view, it will become easy to draw inferences about the reasons for the occurrences of particular phenomena.

Those, on the other hand, who do not welcome such subjects with enthusiasm will not be able to comprehend them and they will not be able to obtain that, for the sake of which we study these subjects <—i.e., peace of mind.>

EPICURUS,

LETTER TO MENEOCEUS

{Diogenes Laertius X.121–135}

FROM Epicurus to Meneoceus: Greetings.

The Importance of Studying Philosophy

Let no one who is young procrastinate when it comes to the study of philosophy; nor, when already old in age, think philosophizing to be burdensome drudgery. Because, when it comes to the health of the soul, it is impossible to be either too young or too old. To say that the right, ripe season for philosophy has not arrived yet, or that it has passed, is the same as to say that the right season for being happy and well has not yet come or is no more.

So, both for young and old, it is imperative to take up the study of philosophy. For the old, so that they may stay youthful even as they are growing older by contemplating the good things <of life> and the <richness of> bygone events. And, for the young, so that they may be like those who are advanced in age in being fearless in the face of what is yet to come.

It is indeed imperative to attend to all those things that produce well-being and happiness. For, when happiness is ours, we have everything; and, when happiness is absent, we do everything to acquire it.

Recommendations for How to Live Well

All those things, which I constantly urge you to do—take action and attend to those, accepting them unquestioningly as essential elements of the proper method for living well and properly.

The Divine

First of all, accept and comprehend that the divine is a living entity, which is indestructible and blessed—a view that is indeed underwritten even by the commonly held view of the divine.

And, never attach to the divine nature any <characteristics> which are incompatible with indestructibility or are not akin to blessedness.

For, gods do exist, as is attested by the fact that we have clear and evident knowledge of them. But the gods are not such as the many take them to be.

For, <consider this:> <if the masses were able to think through the logical consequences that follow from their favored view of divine nature,> they would not be able even to keep those gods alive!

And <don't think that it is> impious to reject the gods of the many. What is impious is actually to adhere to and internalize the common beliefs about the gods.

The claims made by the many about the gods are not rational premises, which are posited first in a proper syllogism; they are rather ad hoc and false assumptions about the gods, which are posited in order to account for facts <which the many are unable to explain.> Hence, <it is a commonly held view that> the greatest harms befalling human beings are penalties inflicted by the gods on evil people—and the parallel belief is held for prosperity's advantages.

<This is inevitable:> Individuals being in all respects familiar with their own views of excellence, they are able to recognize only what is similar to themselves and they regard everything that is dissimilar to themselves as alien.

Death

Develop the habit of thinking that death is nothing to us <human beings;> because everything that is good and bad is in sense perception; but death is the cessation of sense perception. From which it follows that the correct belief is that death is of no significance and is non-existent. This makes life's mortality enjoyable—not by adding an unlimited time span but by removing the frenzied yearning for immortality.

Moreover, for one who has comprehended fully that there is nothing dreadful about not being alive, there can be nothing dreadful in life either.

One who asserts that death ought to be feared is uttering vacuous statements: he is afraid of something that is not going to ever cause grief when it is present but can only cause sadness by being in the future! Because, indeed, it is vacuous to anticipate with sadness anything that cannot bother us when it becomes present.

So, the most horrid of evils—death itself—is nothing of significance to us <human beings:> Because, for as long as we exist, death cannot be present to us; and, when death comes to us, we have by then ceased to exist.

So, death exists neither for those who are alive nor for those who have died: because it is not an actual present thing for the former and the latter do not exist themselves.

Yet the masses flee from death as if it were the gravest of evils. And there are even occasions, on which the many (will actually choose death as a solution to the <presumed> evils and sufferings of life. But one who is wise neither gives up living) nor is afraid of not being alive. Because life is not an encumbrance or burden to him and he does not judge death to be an evil.

It is the same with food: <the person of right judgment> does not choose what is simply and unqualifiedly the largest amount of food; he rather chooses that food which is the most pleasant.

So it is with life's time span: He does not seize the fruit that lasts longer but that which is the most pleasant.

Those who urge the young to live well and the old to. . . die well are nitwits. Not only because life is intrinsically valuable and worthy of being welcomed at all times but also because the study of how to die well is one and the same with the study of how to live well.

And one is even worse than a nitwit if he states that the best thing is never to come into existence or

> *Once born, to pass through the gates of Hades*
> *As quickly as possible.*[1]

If one says such things from conviction, how is it at all possible that he is still alive?

If he has indeed reached this conclusion firmly and as the result of rational deliberation, the further preparations needed for preparing one's death are relatively trivial.

If, on the other hand, he is saying all this to be witty or funny, his utterances make no impression on those who are not in a receptive mood.

One should also keep in mind and always remember the following: the future is not ours in each and every respect; but, it is also true that the future *is* ours in certain respects. <This is important to remember> so that we don't expect the future to arrive inexorably and, consequently, we don't fall into despair because the future is not unconditionally there for us.

Epicurean Ethics

Pleasure and Pain

We must now consider that, of desires, some are by and in accordance with nature, whereas others are without a foundation in nature—they are "empty" desires, as it were.

And, of the desires which are in accordance with nature, some are necessary and others are simply natural <and not necessary.>

And of the necessary <natural> desires, some are necessary for well being and happiness; some are necessary for disencumbering the body from its burdens; and some are necessary for <the preservation of> life itself.

51

A fixed theoretical account of these <kinds of desires> ought to provide knowledge about how to refer every choice and every avoidance to the goals of keeping the body healthy and the soul free of perturbation—because this is indeed the ultimate purpose of a blessed life.

For, we do everything for the sake of being free of pain and mental distress.

As soon as this purpose is fulfilled in every respect, all the tempests of the soul dissolve: the animal does not have a need anymore to wander about haltingly—as when in dire necessity—or to seek supplements to the goods of its body and soul.

For, when we are in pain, we need pleasure simply on account of the fact that pleasure is absent.

And, when we are not in pain, we need pleasure no more.

It is for this reason that we <Epicureans> declare pleasure the beginning-and-principle and the end-and-purpose of living a blessed life.

For, it is pleasure that we come to know as the good that is first and most congenially akin to our human nature; and, in every act of choice or avoidance, we begin and take our bearings from pleasure; and to pleasure we always repair at the end, as to a yardstick and principle, by which we judge every good—<commensurately judging affect by reference to> affect.

And, because pleasure is the original good that is akin to our nature, we do not simply choose any pleasure, but there are occasions involving many pleasures when we foreswear the pleasure: <this we do> when the discomfort that follows is much more intense than the pleasure itself.

And we consider many pains to be better than <certain> pleasures: <this we do> when a greater and more enduring pleasure is expected to supervene after we have endured the pain.

Indeed, every pleasure is a good on account of its natural affinity <with our human nature,> but it does not follow that every pleasure is choice worthy without qualification.

<It is the same with pain:> every pain is an evil, and yet it doesn't follow that our natural inclination is to flee each and every pain unqualifiedly.

It is imperative that we judge all such things by taking into account the comparative measurements of the advantages and disadvantages <that follow from the uses of pleasures and pains.>

And we <Epicureans> think that self-sufficiency is a great good, not in the sense that we should always and in every respect avail ourselves of few things, but so that, if we chance not to have plenty, we might be able to find a few things sufficient. <And this we say> being fully convinced that those who least need luxury are able to relish it most sweetly; and also that it is easy to provide what is in accordance with nature, whereas it is exceedingly difficult to procure what is without a foundation in nature; and that simple brews bring pleasure equal to that of sumptuous feasts insofar as they remove the entire pain <of privation;> and bread and water yield the highest pleasure to one who is brought to them after he has been in dire necessity.

Becoming habituated in the simple—and abjuring the sumptuous—diet is a fundamental component of good health and makes a human being capable of combating sloth and inertia in the face of life's hardships; and predisposes us more effectively to handle luxury when we come to it from a long interval <of privation;> and makes us fearless in the face of inscrutable fortune.

And when we say that the natural end-state and ultimate purpose consists in pleasure, we are not speaking of the pleasures of the profligate or those pleasures which depend on <unqualified> enjoyment—as some claim <that we do,> either from ignorance <of our teachings,> disagreement, or calumnious intent.

We are rather speaking of a state in which the body is free of pain and the soul is free of distress.

For it is neither the partaking of drinking binges and shameless banquets, the enjoyment of young boys and women, nor the fish and such goodies of the sumptuous table that produce a pleasant life; but it is rather sober deliberation <that produces

a pleasant life>—that deliberation which inquires into and ferrets out the <deeper> reasons behind every choice and every avoidance and expels all those opinions which fill the soul with the greatest perturbations.

Prudence

In relation to all these things, prudence is the proper principle and greatest good. This is the reason that prudence is even more precious than philosophy itself. It is from prudence that all the other virtues [excellences] follow according to nature.

Prudence teaches that it is impossible to live pleasantly without leading a life of moderation, honorable civility, and justice; and that it is impossible to live such a life without living pleasantly.

Because the virtues [excellences] are by nature entwined with the pleasant life and the pleasant life is itself inseparable from the virtues [excellences].

For, who, do you think, can be better than one who holds pious views about the gods, is fearless in every respect in the face of the death, has reasoned notions about the proper purpose of life, and realizes that the natural limit of good things is easy to reach and provide for and that the limit of bad things either has brief duration or merely mild pains?

•Fate and Chance

As for Fate, who is introduced by some as if she were the sovereign of all, <this is what one ought to say:> (Some things happen of necessity, some by chance, and some through our own voluntary actions. Regarding those things which happen of necessity, the human agent is not responsible; regarding chance, it is easy to see that she is unstable; but what is due to our own voluntary actions—that is free and not subject to any higher sovereign: indeed, it is because of this <freedom> that it is sensible to speak of assigning responsibility and meting out punishments and rewards to moral agents.)

For it would be better to even dovetail the fairy tales about the gods than to be a slave to the Fate of certain philosophers of nature. Because the former <i.e., belief in the myths about gods> promote the hope that one might be able to gain release by honoring the gods; whereas the latter <Fate> represents necessity as unexceptional and inescapable.

And one should not consider chance to be a god, as the many do—because a god does nothing in a disorderly manner. Nor should one consider Fate to be an uncertain natural cause.

One should not think that the good and bad things, which contribute to living a blessed life, are provided by chance—although, indeed, the origins of good and bad things may be from chance.

It is, at any rate, better to come to bad luck after one has deliberated properly than to become happy by chance after one has been unreasonable. Because, in human affairs, it is better that the outcome of good deliberation (is not corrected by chance than that poor judgment) is set straight by chance.

Conclusion

Study and pay attention, day and night, to all these things to those related to them, both by yourself and in the company of others like you, and nothing will ever disturb you either when you are awake or when you are asleep; and you will live like a god among human beings. For a human being, insofar as he is alive, is in no respect like the mere mortal animals if he only dwells in the midst of immortal goods.

EPICURUS,

PRINCIPAL DOCTRINES

{Diogenes Laertius, X.139-154}

THAT which is blessed and indestructible has no affairs of its own to attend to; nor does it inflict any trouble on others. So, it is agitated neither by ire nor by partiality. For all such are to be found in that which lacks power.

Death is nothing to us. Because, what has been dissolved has no sense perception; and, according to us, what has no sense perception is nothing to worry about.

Pleasure has its <upper> limit in the removal of everything that produces pain. For, wherever that which produces pleasure resides, for as long as it abides, there can be nothing that produces pain, grief, or both.

What produces pain does not remain constantly in the body over a long period of time; it is rather that the maximal pain persists for the least span of time, and even that bodily pain which barely exceeds pleasure does not continue to happen for many days <in a row.> And, indeed, chronic illnesses themselves have an excess of what produces bodily pleasure over what is productive of pain.

It is impossible to lead a pleasant life without leading a life that is prudent, proper, and just. Nor is it possible to live a life that is prudent, proper, and just without living a life that is pleasant. Whoever lacks <any one of> the above <elements of a good and pleasant life> cannot have a good life.

This <human ability to lead a good life> originally became possible by nature and for the sake of imparting courage in human beings <who were then living in a pre-social condition.> And this is the natural origin and principle on which all authority—be it even kingship—is based. And it is from the same <natural propensities> that a human being is able also to arrange a good and pleasant life.

Some have wished to become famous and enviable, thinking that they would in this way procure for themselves security from other human beings. In that case: if their life is secure, they have indeed enjoyed what is the good by nature; if, however, they are not safe, they still lack that naturally familiar good for the sake of which our appetites have striven from the very first stirrings of human nature and in accordance with natural principles.

No pleasure is a morally bad thing in itself. But the agents that produce certain pleasures bring about vexations that outnumber the pleasures themselves.

If all pleasures could be added together consecutively with respect to space and duration, and across the entire span over which they had all existed, or at least across the principal parts of human nature <which are naturally susceptible to pleasures:> then, pleasures would not be different from each other in any respect.

If those elements that are productive of the pleasures of the debauched released them from the mental apprehensions aroused by natural phenomena, fear of death, and <obsessive anticipation of> pain; if, in addition, they formed their characters in such a way that they knew when to set a limit to their desires, we would then never have anything to censure them about: indeed, they would then be fully actualizing all the pleasures and in no way would they have either what is painful or what is productive of grief in them—and it is this latter condition <which they would be avoiding> that is morally bad.

If we were never perturbed by frightful second-guessing of natural phenomena and death; if, adding to the above, we were never <beset by> failure to comprehend the proper limits of pains and pleasures: then, we would have no need of natural science.

It is impossible to be released from fear about the most important things for one who, not having adequate knowledge as to what the nature of the whole is, is trying to second-guess this or that in accordance with the <traditional> fairy tales. Hence, it is impossible to enjoy the pleasures in full unless one has studied natural science.

There is generally no benefit in procuring safety and protection from other human beings when one lives constantly in frightful conjecture about what is over our heads and those that are under the earth and those that simply are, without qualification, in boundless space.

Although safety from human beings may be secured, up to a point, by means of bountiful resources and power that can exempt one from <some risks;> yet, the most genuine safety comes from leading a tranquil private life and keeping aloof from the masses.

The bounty of nature is not only easy to extract as a resource; it also has its own limits set <by nature> <so that one cannot run into excess insofar as he is attuned to nature;> but the opulence of hollow fancies plunges precipitously into a space that has no limits.

The wise are rarely infringed by chance; the matters that are most significant and decisive have been, are, and always will be governed by reason throughout the entire span of a wise person's life.

The just person is the most imperturbable; but the unjust is filled with ample distress.

Bodily pleasure cannot increase anymore once all the pain produced by need has been removed, even if this happened for the first time; <after that point, additional> pleasure can only <accrue from> variation. But the limit of the pleasure produced by mental pursuits is generally attained by means of reflecting on all those things, and on others kindred to the things, which furnish the mind with the greatest frights.

Time without limit affords the same amount of pleasure as does limited time—if one measures the limits of pleasure precisely and by using reasoned judgment.

The body picks out the end points of pleasure as lying beyond any limit, and marks the time needed to procure this <pleasure> as being unlimited. But the mind, grasping the final goal and terminating limits of the body by means of comprehending judgment, and obliterating the dread of an eternal afterlife, makes possible a life that reaches all goals within itself and has no need whatever of infinite time. But it should not <be thought> that the mind flees from pleasure—not even at that moment when circumstances bring about the extraction from this life—or that it destroys the pleasures as if they were unworthy of the best life.

He who knows well the limits of living also knows that to remove pain caused by need is easy—resources for that are not lacking—so that one's entire life can be rendered complete and replete with all possible purposes. It follows that there is no need whatever of things unless they are won by noble struggle.

When all is said and done, we need to take into account what kinds of things exist in the universe and every vivid and clear sense perception, to which we must refer opinions; if we fail to do so, everything will be full of gullibility and confusion.

If you wage battle against all the sensations, <not only will you lose those you are directly fighting against but, also> you won't even have those sensations left, by reference to which alone you could claim to have won your case.

If you expel each and every sensation without qualification, and fail to draw <fitting> distinctions applying to what is opined <about sensations> as between what is present already and what is anticipated; or if you fail to draw distinctions applying to what is opined <about sensations> as to whether such opinions are according to sense perception, the passions, or some other imaginary twist of mind: you will, then, confound also the rest of your sensations <in addition to the ones you are trying to expel directly> because of this ineffective way of judging, so that you will also have expelled all criteria for judging what is true and what is false.

If you don't judge every one of your actions by reference to the end and goal dictated by nature, in accordance also with the proper natural timing for each action, but, instead, second guessing <nature,> you veer off ahead of time attempting either to pursue or to flee <goals,> then your acts will not be turning out to be consistent with your rationalizations.

Of desires, those which do not bring one to pain if they remain unfulfilled are not necessary; such desires are actually accompanied by appetites that are easily defused: indeed, <this is evidently what happens> when it is thought difficult to find the means to satisfy <unnecessary desires> or when the desires themselves are thought to be productive of harm.

Of all those things by means of which wisdom can procure blessed bliss to last for an entire life, by far the greatest is the acquisition of friends.

The same (judgment) which enables us to wax confident in contemplating that no dreadful thing is eternal, or even of long duration, also knows well that, in these our constrained circumstances, security depends on having friends more than on anything else.

Of desires, some are natural and (necessary; some are natural and) not necessary; some are neither natural nor necessary and are only created by empty belief.

Certain natural desires, which do not reduce one to pain if they are not satisfied, have, nevertheless, a commensurate inherent need for satisfaction. Such desires are born, indeed, of empty belief: the reason they are not defused is not to be traced to their intrinsic nature but to the person's vacuity.

Natural justice is an expression of the <natural> interest <everyone has> and consists in both: a) not causing harm to others, and b) not suffering harm for oneself.

Some animals are incapable of entering into compacts that agree not to inflict harm in order to avoid suffering harm: in the cases of such animals neither moral right nor moral wrong can be said to apply. Similarly, there are communities which are either incapable or unwilling to make treaties that undertake not to inflict harm in order to avoid suffering harm: <in the cases of such communities, the concepts of moral right and moral wrong cannot be said to apply either.>

Abstract justice in itself does not exist. Justice rather <comes into being only> in instances of reciprocal intercourse, applies specifically to this or that place <and time,> and consists in a covenanted agreement to refrain from inflicting harm for the sake of not having harm inflicted on oneself.

Injustice is not a moral evil in itself: what is bad about injustice consists in the wearying apprehension that one might fail to escape detection by those who mete out punishments.

And it is not possible for someone to be confident that he will not be detected if one has acted surreptitiously in violating any one of the provisions of the social contract, which consists in <an agreement> to refrain from harming for the sake of avoiding harm for oneself; not even if one has escaped detection a myriad times until the present: for even to the moment of one's final demise, there can be no sure sign or assurance that one will continue to escape detection.

Generally speaking, justice is one and the same for all: i.e., justice is something or other that is to one's interest in mutual intercourse. But, speaking on a case-by-case basis, justice is not the same for all as it depends on <specific> regions and factors.

Among those things that are conventionally accepted as just, whatever is universally acknowledged to be conducive to the purpose of maintaining civic society is necessarily adjudged to be a patently just thing, whether it is the same for all people or not.

But if one stipulates something as the law even though it is at cross purposes with the interest of maintaining civic society—such an ordinance does not partake of natural justice in any way.

In addition, if and to the extent that the interests which are in accordance with natural justice prove variable, so that concepts of justice can remain harmonious with natural interests only for a certain period of time: we must say that such concepts of justice <though short-lived> are no less just within their corresponding frames of time.

<This is what we must say> if we are not to perturb ourselves with hollow words but rather take our bearings from the truth about human affairs.

In those instances, in which, without any new developments arising, it becomes evident that the accepted concepts of justice are not, after all, in harmony with concrete interests or exertions of human effort: we must, in such cases, admit that those concepts of justice have had nothing to do with justice to begin with.

But, in those instances, in which novel developments make it disadvantageous to preserve the same <concepts of> justice: in such cases, we must say that the concepts of justice were true in the past, for as long as they were conducive to the mutual association of fellow citizens, but, subsequently, when they were no longer advantageous, they were no longer just to adhere to.

He who was fittingly constituted in such a way that he could not face up to external dangers prepared a family made up of as many kindred beings as he was able to bring together; or, those he could not bring together, he related to as if they were not, at any rate, members of a different species. And with those beings, which he was altogether unable <either to bring into a family or to relate to in any way,> he did not mingle at all and, to the extent that it was to his benefit to do so, he had nothing to do with them.

Those who had the greatest ability to prepare defenses against their neighbors, so they could face up to them, were the ones who lived with each most pleasantly—since they had the most certain guarantee <that they were in no danger in any respect.> And, given that they had once enjoyed the most complete intimacy, they would not lament or cry for mercy if one suffered a premature demise.

EPICURUS,

LETTER TO IDOMENEUS

USENER 138 = DL 22

Greetings to Idomeneus from Epicurus

Leading the last and blessedly joyous day of life, already coming to an end, this very letter I have written to you.
Truly, this has come to pass following urinary and intestinal afflictions that have been lacking nothing in their excessive severity. But to all these stood opposed the cheerfulness of a soul rejoicing in the memory of the meditations she had ever birthed. And you, proving worthy of your association with me—ever since you were a young boy—take good care of the children of Metrodorus.

SHORT FRAGMENTS AND TESTIMONIA (UNCERTAIN AUTHENTICITY)

On the Value of Philosophy

U 221 = Porphyry, *Ad Marcellam* 31

A philosophy which cannot heal any one of the maladies afflicting human beings is empty. This is not unlike the case of medicine: It is of no benefit whatsoever unless it can effectively expel illness from the human body. So it is with philosophy too: It is of no worth whatever unless it can expel the ailments of the soul.

On the Study of Philosophy and on Philosophers

U 238 = Diogenes Laertius X.8

Epicurus was in the habit of calling all those who used to hobnob with Plato "flatterers of tyrants." Moreover, Epicurus considered the Cynics enemies of Greece and the dialecticians prolific. . . corruptors. As for Pyrrho, Epicurus thought of him as illiterate and uneducated.

U 240 = Diogenes Laertius X.12

Diocles says that Epicurus, first and foremost, accepted Anaxagoras as a great thinker, even though he disagreed with him in certain respects. Also, Epicurus accepted the teachings of Archytas, the teacher of Socrates.

On Sense Perception

U 244 = Sextus, *Adversus Mathematicos* 8.9

Epicurus considered all sense data to be true and truly exis-tent. Because there is no difference between something being said to be true and something being in existence. Hence, briefly outlining the concepts of true and false, Epicurus says: that is true which is as it is said to be; and that is false which is not as it is said to be.

U 248 = Aetius IV.9.5

Epicurus considers every sense datum and every product of the mind's exertions, which is based on sense data, to be true; but of beliefs he thought that some are true and some are false...

U 246 = Diogenes Laertius X.106

According to the Skeptics all the evidence we can possibly have consists in what something appears to be. Epicurus agrees with this too. [The appearance is the ultimate criterion of truth.]

U 247 = Sextus VII.203–216

Epicurus claims that there are two, mutually conjoined, things: imagination <mental exertion that depends only on material that is already in the mind> and belief <about external objects and events;> of these two he considers imagination to be always and in every respect true; he even calls imagination "crystal clear." The most basic affections, such as pleasure and pain, are constituted by certain characteristic productive factors and in ways that are always consistent with these active factors: i.e., pleasure is always produced by what is pleasant and pain by what is painful, and there is no chance ever that what produces pleasure is not itself pleasant or that what bestows pain is not itself painful; rather, it is necessarily true that what pleases is pleasant and what gives pain is painful in its very nature. Similarly, what produces mental affects is, through and through and in every respect, an object of the mind's operations; and it follows that mental constructs which comprise the imagination cannot fail to exist <as it is thought of.> *** And we need to think how this applies in each similar case. For instance, what is being seen not only appears to be such and such but it is also such as it appears to be. And what is being heard does not only sound as if it were like this or that but it is indeed always such as it sounds.

And the same applies equally in all similar cases.

Likewise, all mental representations <including figments of the imagination> turn out to be true; and it is only logical that this would be so.

This is what Epicurus says to prove the above contentions: a mental representation is <by definition> true when it comes into existence from something that is already in existence and in strict accordance with this existent thing. But every successive mental construct comes into existence from a prior, already existent, mental construct and is constituted strictly in accordance with this prior mental construct. Therefore, every mental construct is necessarily true.

Some are deceived by the fact that there is a difference between something being perceived—for instance, being seen—and the evidently modified mental representations which are triggered by this initially perceived sensible: this is a process, by means of which the original visible entity now appears in a mental construct and is altered in shape or color or in any other respect. Because of this, the point is often made that, given that we now have several differentiated and mutually inconsistent mental representations, it must necessarily be the case that one of them is true and its contraries are necessarily false. This, however, is nonsense! Only those who fail to have a synoptic view of the ultimate natures that are inherent in things can be deceived into offering this critique.

To give an example involving things that we see: a solid object cannot be seen in its entirety; only the color of the solid is seen. And, as far as the color is concerned, some of the color is in the solid object itself, as is the case with objects we look at from close up or from a relatively short distance; and some of the color is outside the solid and in the places which effectively impinge on the solid place, as it seems when we look at the solid object from a sufficiently long distance. The color changes and successively assumes different configurations—each one peculiar to each place—so that it gives rise to corresponding <and correspondingly differentiated> mental representations. And, so, each mental construct *is* true relative to its corresponding configuration <of color-in-place.> The same happens with sound: the sound that is heard is not the same as that in the bronze that was struck or in the mouth of the person who shouted; the sound that is heard is rather the sound that impinges on our <organ of> sense perception.

Now, we would not say of someone who heard a sound from a distance and claimed that he had heard a soft sound that he was lying—because he then heard, again, a loud sound when he went near: by the same token, we should not say that someone was lying with regard to visible appearance if he said that he saw the tower as small and round from a distance but, from close up, he saw it as large and rectangular. We should rather say that he was speaking truthfully on both occasions.

In other words, whenever the sense stimulus appears to be small and of this or that shape, it is indeed true that the <perceived> stimulus is truly small and of this or that shape. This happens because the edges of the images that are emitted from things are shattered off due to the fact that they are carried far through the air. And, again, for the opposite reason, something can be seen as large and of a different shape <when seen from close up.> Indeed, it is *not* the same object that is impinging on our organ of sense perception on both occasions.

It is indeed characteristic of a distorted opinion to think that it has been the same sensible that was seen both from close up and from a distance. {So, again, it is opinion and not the immediate sense perception that leads to falsehood.}

What is unique to sense perception on each occasion is what is present to and impinging on <the organ of> sense perception in each case—setting sense perception in motion. But what would make sense perception distinguish because this or that present object is never present to it.

For this reason, all mental representations <including figments of the imagination> that directly refer to the stimuli are true <whereas beliefs, on the other hand, may be true or false.> Mental constructs are true even if they offer different assessments <of the same object or situation.>

On the other hand, of beliefs, some are true and some are false. This is because beliefs establish judgments about, and assessments of, the mental representations: we judge some things correctly and some things badly either by adding and attributing something to a mental construct or by subtracting and withdrawing something from a mental construct—i.e., generally, by contradicting the pre-rational sense perception.

Therefore, in sum, according to Epicurus, some beliefs are true and some are false: those beliefs are true which are confirmed *and* fail to be falsified by "crystal clear" perceptions; and those beliefs are false which are disconfirmed *and* are not corroborated by the "crystal clear" perceptions.

Confirmation consists in reaching the firm conclusion, by means of comparison with crystal clear perceptions, that what was taken as being a certain thing is indeed what it had been thought to be. As, for example, when Plato is approaching from afar, was considered as being Plato but only as a matter of belief, considering the distance from which he was seen; and, while he was passing by, after he had come near, it was confirmed by means of crystal clear and accurate sense perceptions that it was indeed Plato.

And what constitutes "absence of disconfirmation" is the existence of logical agreement between the phenomenon that has been established through sense perception and the non-evident thing that is being believed without being experienced directly. For example, when Epicurus says that the void—or empty space—exists: even though it is invisible, the void is confirmed—or not disconfirmed—to exist by means of Epicurus' argument about motion {that motion would be impossible without empty space}. Now, motion is something that is crystal clear: it is undeniable that motion takes place. According to this argument, if no empty space existed, it would be necessarily impossible for motion to ever take place: as everything would be filled out and as the plenum would be perfectly dense, a <presumably> moving body could find no place into which it could move. So, even though empty space cannot be evident to the senses, on the other hand it is true that no contrary evidence [to the existence of empty space] is offered by the phenomena which we do experience. . . .

From all this it follows that:

a) availability of confirming evidence and lack of disconfirming evidence are criteria which establish that something is true; whereas

b) lack of confirming evidence and availability of disconfirming evidence are criteria which establish that something is false.

Confirmation and disconfirmation are the pillars and foundation <of the method for ascertaining truth and falsehood of claims.>

U 247.20–27

Epicurus used to say that all sense data are always true and truly in existence. This he said because he drew no distinction between saying-that-something-is-true and something-being-truly-in-existence. . . . And he considered sense perception to be mere receptivity with respect to those things that impinge upon it—so that, he thought, sense perception would neither add, subtract, nor qualify anything because sense perception, by itself, is not rational. So, Epicurus thought, sense perception always introduces truths and receives beings exactly as they are by nature. While sense data are always true, beliefs may be either true or false.

U 247.28-36

Of the natural philosophers, some, like Democritus, denied that any appearances are true, whereas others, like Epicurus, accepted all appearances as being true. . . .

U 253 = Sextus Empiricus, *Adversus Mathematicos* VIII.63–64

Epicurus used to say that all sense data are always true and that every mental construct is triggered by something that exists, and is exactly of the same kind as that which set the organ of sense perception into motion. Those who say that some mental representations are true and some false are mistaken. They fall into this error because they are unable to distinguish belief from crystal-clear mental representations. Take for instance the case of Orestes—when it seemed to him that he was seeing the Furies: insofar as this was indeed put into motion by images, his sense perception was truthful—for those images did exist! It was only when his mind formed the belief that the Furies were in fact solid beings that he was forming a false opinion.

And, says Epicurus, the philosophers who deny all this will never be able to convince us that some of these sense data are true and some are false by introducing, as they are apt to do, additional distinctions among different mental representations. They will not be able to prove this either by means of appearances (because it is appearance that we are investigating in the first place <and, hence, are not at liberty to assume that we already know enough about appearances>); nor can they convince us by referring to what is non-evident (because the non-evident must be argued about on the basis of premises that are derived from appearances).

On Nature

U 266

Nothing new can be added to the whole universe, for it is already complete given that the time that has elapsed so far is infinite.

On Atoms

U 267 = Aetius I.3

Epicurus the Athenian, son of Neocles, philosophizing as a Democritean, said that the building blocks of beings are bodies which are apprehended only by means of reasoning; such bodies do not partake of the void <i.e., admit no empty space;> they are without a beginning, indestructible, and cannot be crushed; nor can they have any parts rearranged or altered in any way. . . .

And these bodies move in empty space and through empty space. This empty space is without limit and the number of these solid bodies is infinite. These bodies are called atoms <i.e., indivisibles or uncuttables>—not in the sense that they are of minimum size but in the sense that they cannot be cut any further since they cannot be affected in any way and are unable to partake of empty space. . . .

U 268 = Simplicius on Aristotle, *Physics* Z.1, beginning.

Those who became aware of the impossibility of subdividing bodies ad infinitum—i.e., that we cannot possibly keep subdividing extended bodies forever—concluded that bodies must be ultimately subdivided only down to indivisibles. Except that Leucippus and Democritus did not confine themselves to taking this inability <of those bodies> to be affected in any way as the basic property of first elements, but also added, as properties, small size and lack of parts.

Later, Epicurus did not consider the first elements to be without parts but said that these are *atoms* merely on account of their inherent inability to be affected in any way. Epicurus did this because Aristotle had scrutinized and decisively criticized the views about first elements held by Leucippus and Democritus. And, perhaps bearing in mind that Aristotelian critique of the claim that first elements have no parts, even as he sympathized with the atomic theory of Leucippus and Democritus, Epicurus preserved the view that those first elements are unable to be affected in any way but omitted the claim that they do not have any parts.

On Motion and Change

U 291 = Sextus Empiricus, *Adversus Mathematicos* X.42

Some of the natural philosophers, Epicurus being one of them, said that the motion whereby things change is one particular type of the process whereby things move from one place to another: because the admixture which undergoes qualitative changes, always and in every respect, according to and because of the transpositional motion of its constituents. And we are to identify those constituents by reasoning about them. For example, when something changes and becomes bitter after it has initially been sweet, or black after it has been white—for this to happen it must needs be the case that its constituent masses have shifted around so that their relative order and arrangements have changed and received new ordering structures. And this could not happen in any other way except by the masses moving from place to place <relative to each other.>

Similarly, again, for something to become soft after it has been hard, or hard after it has been soft, it must needs be the case that the particles, of which it is made up, have moved from place to place. Indeed, when the particles move apart, a thing becomes soft; and when they gather closer together, it becomes hard.

From all this it follows that the motion whereby change is effectuated is not different, in genus, from the motion by means of which something moves from one place to another.

Time

U 294 = Sextus Empiricus, *Adversus Mathematicos* X.219–227.

As Demetrius the Lacon explains, Epicurus says that time is an accident which happens to another accident. Time follows days and nights and hours and affects and absence of affect and motion and rest. Because all these things are accidents that happen to befall someone; and time happens to be attached to and attendant upon all the above-mentioned accidents. So, it makes sense to say that time is an accident of accidents.

On Space

U 297 = Simplicius, Commentary on Aristotle's *Physics* 203b20.

A fourth point, which we should not ignore, is that everything that has boundaries is evidently always extending up to, and in contact with, what demarcates and delimits it. Because if something that has boundaries were delimited by something else which is external to it, then this outside thing would have to be itself either with or without boundaries: If without boundaries, then we have already come across the infinitely extended here. If, on the other hand, <this external delimiting thing> were to be itself delimited (as the earth is), then this too must be delimited by something else, and so on ad infinitum. If this were indeed to go on without end, then <once again it is shown that> the infinite has true existence: because we will never be able to find the ultimate boundary since this presumed ultimate boundary would also need to be delimited by something else.

As Alexander says, it was especially those around Epicurus who gave credence to this argument: so, they would say that the whole is unlimited or infinitely extended—because everything that is delimited is bounded by something else, which also has an external boundary, <and so on, ad infinitum.>

Aristotle actually mentions this argument too—which indicates that the argument goes back to times long before Epicurus.

Alexander Aphrodisias, *Questions* III.12.200.20.

And those who say, in opposition, that, for everything that is delimited, its boundary must be external to it: they have a point if we accept that being delimited is a condition which inheres in something only when we consider this something against the background of something else. . . .

On Empty Space or the Void

U 272 = Sextus Empiricus, *Adversus Mathematicos* VIII.239

Epicurus believes that he has presented the most powerful proof that empty space exists: if there is motion, empty space must necessarily exist; but there clearly is motion; therefore, empty space exists.

U 301 = Galenus, *De animi peccatorum distinctione et curatione* c.7.

The Stoics consider the void as something that is not internal to the universe. Rather, the Stoic takes the void to be something that is outside the universe. Epicurus, on the other hand, brings the two <universe and the void> together, in one place as it were. And this is not the only respect in which Epicurus disagrees <with the Stoics.> Unlike the Stoics, who in agreement with the Peripatetics in this respect aver that only one world exists, Epicurus admits an infinite number of worlds. According to Epicurus, as the void is unbounded, so there is an infinite number of worlds in it.

U301a = Aetius, II.1.8.329b3D.

Epicurus considers the intervening spaces between worlds to be unequal in length.

U 302 = Aetius, II.2.3.329a5D.

Epicurus says that it is possible that worlds may be spherical but that it is also possible that they may have any one of many other geometrical shapes.

U 303 = Aetius, II.7.3.336D.

Epicurus thought that the boundary <or outlying region> of some worlds is rarefied while the boundary of others is dense. He also says that the boundaries of some worlds are in motion while the boundaries of others are at rest.

On the Formation of Our World

U 308* = pseudo-Plutarch, *de placitis philos.* I.4.

This present world came together, formed in its present shape with bent edges, in the following way: the atoms are bodies which have motion inherent to them; this motion is unpremeditated and random. It is also the case that the atoms move constantly and without interruption; and they move with extremely high velocities. In this way, many bodies were assembled—bodies of various shapes, sizes, and weights. As they were being assembled in this fashion, those bodies which happened to be larger in size and heavier settled further down than the rest; and those bodies which happened to be smaller in size, rounded in shape, and easily mobile, smooth, or slippery were squeezed out by the gathering concourse of atoms and were tossed upwards into the higher region. And, as the force of the impact which had thrown them upward began to diminish, the shock would no longer carry them to the upper region; at the same time, they were also blocked and prevented from any downward movement: so, they were pressed into the place which could receive them; those were the places which surrounded the main concourse of atoms; and into these places the multitudes of bodies were finally thrown—broken all around <which allowed them to fit snugly.> As they became entangled with each other during this process, they gave birth to the sky.

Even though they all have the same nature, the atoms are also varied, as has been said. As they were pushed out toward the upper region, the atoms came to compose the stuff of which celestial bodies are naturally made.

The multitudes of the bodies which had evaporated <during this process> would then keep smiting the air and squeezing it out; the air then turned into yet more rarefied stuff and, still moving about, came to encompass and contain all the celestial bodies, carrying them along with its own motion and, in this way, setting them in their orbits, which we observe currently.

And, subsequently, from the bodies which had settled down the earth was born. And from the bodies in the upper region, the sky and the air and fire were born.

A great amount of matter had been still left on the earth. As this matter condensed under the blows of the bodies and hit by the luminous impacts of the celestial bodies, the earth's entire arrangement was pressed and squeezed together. This could happen because earthly matter was composed of small parts and, in this way, could generate the liquid nature. As it has the propensity to flow, liquid nature was then carried downward by its own momentum; so it moved toward the hollow places and, particularly, toward those places which were able to contain and encompass water. Or, maybe, it was the case that the water itself, and by itself, rendered the underlying places hollow. The principal parts of the world were generated in the above-mentioned fashion.

On the Soul

U 311 = Scholion on Epicurus' Epistle I.66.

Epicurus says that the soul is, in certain respects, composed of atoms which are most smooth and perfectly spherical; and such atoms are, in many respects, different from those that compose fire. One part of the soul is irrational and it is this part that is seeded throughout the rest of the body. The other part of the soul is rational and is lodged in the chest, as evidenced by the fact that such affects as fear and joy are located there. . . .

U 312 = Aetius IV.4.6.390D.

Democritus and Epicurus consider the soul to be bipartite: one part has the ability to reason and is established in the chest; the other is irrational and is seeded throughout the entire composition which is the body.

U 315 = Aetius IV.3.11.388D.

Epicurus considers the soul to be a mixture of four things: a certain fire-like kind of stuff; an air-like kind of stuff; a kind that is rarefied; and a fourth kind of thing which cannot be named. And he took this to be the means by which sense perception is made possible.

From the above-named components of the soul: the rarefied stuff imparts motion; the air-like stuff imparts rest; the warm imparts the heat which is in evidence in a living body; and the unnamed stuff imparts the sense perception which we have in us—because sense perception does not reside in any one of the named constituents of the soul.

On Sense Perception

U 317 = Aetius IV.8.10.

Leucippus, Democritus, and Epicurus said that sense perception and thinking are constituted of images which arrive from outside. For no sense perception data and no thought ever befall anyone without an accompanying image which impinges from outside.

U 319 = Alexander Aphrodisias, Commentary on Aristotle's "On the Senses," 438a5ff.

Democritus, and, before him, Leucippus and, later, the Epicureans thought that the things that are seen are certain images which flow off from things and are of similar form as the things from which they emanate. The sense of vision becomes possible when such images impinge on the eyes of those who see. As proof of this they advanced the following: it is always the case that, in the pupils of the eyes of those who are looking at something, there is an inner appearance and reflected image of what is being seen: from which it is evident that "seeing" is exactly this process.

U 321 = Aetius IV.19.2.408D.

Epicurus considers sound to be a current that is sent off by those who are shouting, making any kind of noise, or hitting surfaces. And this current is discontinuously constituted of shattered particles of similar shape. ("Similar shape" is understood in the sense in which circular shapes, for instance, are said to be similar to other spherical shapes; or in the way triangles are found to be similar to other triangles of the same type.) When those particles impinge <on the organ of hearing,> the sense perception of hearing is produced.

Proof of this is furnished by the letting out of air from bags and by the sound made by air which is made to blow through garments.

U 322

Epicurus, Democritus, and the Stoics consider sound to be material body.

On Generation and Procreation

U 329 = Aetius V.3.5.417D

Epicurus says that the seed is a fragment of the body and of the soul.

U 330 = Aetius V.5.1.418D.

Pythagoras, Epicurus, and Democritus say that the female also produces seed. For, they say, the female also has seed-producing organs, which are turned inwards. And it is this fact that explains how the female too can have a sexual appetite.

U 332 = Aetius V.16.426D.

Democritus and Epicurus say that the fetus, while in the womb, receives nourishment through the mouth. So, upon being born, it immediately offers the mouth to the nipple. And they also said that in the womb too there are nipples and openings through which the fetus receives nourishment.

On Eloqution

U 334 = Origenes, *Contra Celsum* I.24.

The subject concerning the nature of words is profound and obscure. Is Aristotle right in claiming that words are posited by conventional agreement? Or is it rather, as Epicurus teaches, in disagreement with the Stoics, that words are posited in accordance with nature? According to the latter, the first human beings let out certain sounds in imitation of the sounds made by objects.

U 335 = Proclus, On the *Cratylus* 16.

Pythagoras and Epicurus had the same view as Cratylus. Epicurus thought that words derive their significations in accordance with nature: i.e., he thought that the relevant natural processes are prior to <and led to> the naming of objects. In this view, naming objects is not different from the natural correspondences between "seeing" and "what is being seen" or between "hearing" and "sound." Similarly, words are also by nature—they are products of natural processes. . . .

So, Epicurus said that those who posited words for the first time did not do so because they were actuated by advanced knowledge but rather because they were subject to certain natural processes. This is in evidence in the case of those who <make utterances because they are compelled to> cough, sneeze, bellow, howl, or sigh.

On Death and Mortality

U 336 = Aetius IV.7.4.393D.

Epicurus and Democritus considered the soul to be destructible: it perishes along with the body <or simultaneously with the dissolution of the union that comprises the soul and the body.>

U 337 = Sextus *Adversus Mathematicos*, IX.72.

Epicurus said that, when released from the body, the soul is dispersed and scattered like smoke.

Stobaeus 924H.

If the soul is seeded and preserved within the body like air contained in a bag; or if the soul is mixed together with the body and is being carried about like the smithereens we see wafted by the air through door openings: in that case, it is obvious that the soul would be able to exit from the body and, escaping, it would change its composition and disperse—as Democritus and Epicurus claim.

U 339

We are able to provide security and erect defenses with respect to everything else: but, thanks to death, all human beings <are equal> in that we are all like dwellers in a city without protective walls or fortifying ramparts.

U 340 = Hippolytus 22.5.572.14D.

Epicurus submits that the souls of human beings are co-dissolved along with their bodies—in the same manner in which the souls are co-born along with the bodies. Because the soul is indeed a vital liquid, upon whose departure from the body the entire human being perishes. From which it follows that there are no judgments of the dead and no seated tribunals in Hades. Therefore, one is, in every respect, completely free of responsibility for whatever one does in this life and manages to escape detection.

On the Nature of the Deities

U 355 = Aetius I.7.34.

Epicurus says that the gods have human-like appearances but can be perceived only by means of reasoning due to the fact that the images they exude have exceedingly fine parts.

U 357 = Sextus, *Adversus Mathematicos* IX.178.

But if a god is capable of uttering sounds, he must have organs which permit him to have a voice—organs like lungs and windpipe and tongue and mouth. This, however, is preposterous and akin to Epicurean mythology.

U 359

Generally speaking, there is no advance knowledge or guiding fate in the universe; but everything happens automatically and by itself. This is also explained by the fact that the gods are situated in the regions which Epicurus calls the beyond-worlds. In other words, Epicurus placed the abode of the gods outside the worlds. Epicurus also said that the gods enjoy the greatest degree of bliss that is possible and that they abide in perfect tranquility; and he said that the gods have no business to attend to and no reasons to burden anyone with any tasks.

U 361

According to Epicurus, both Anaxagoras and Plato committed a blunder in making the divine pay attention to human affairs and in saying that the divine fashioned the world for the sake and benefit of human beings. Such a blessed and indestructible entity— one, moreover, who is filled with every kind of good thing and unreceptive to any type of harm and evil—would be naturally preoccupied completely with the task of ensuring continuation of his own happiness and indestructibility; therefore, such a god would have no interest in human affairs. Indeed, such a god would think it bad luck and outright unpleasant if he were to yoke himself like a beast of burden and take minute care in fashioning this world—in the manner, as it were, of a common laborer!

U 363 = Plutarch, *Pyrri* 20.

The Epicureans exile the divine beyond benevolence, wrath, and providence, to a way of life that is altogether idle and vainly seasoned by the pleasures of a voluptuary.

U 364

It is as if this Epicurus had managed to leave the world behind and jumped over the celestial circumference itself! Or, perhaps, he exited through some secret gates, of which he was the only one to know, and, once in the void, he was able to behold the gods themselves and marvel at the blessed indulgences!

And, having on this account waxed desirous of such bliss and having grown emulous of such sumptuous diets-in-the-void, Epicurus exhorts us all to become like those gods so that we too can partake of such blessedness. . . .

U 368 = Lucianus, *bis. Accus.* 2.

Epicurus shows immediately who he really is by saying that the gods have no providential care of human affairs. The Epicureans commit supreme blasphemy and are immodest in their religious theories—especially when they say that the gods take no providential care of human affairs and have no cognizance of all that happens.

U 368 = Plutarch, *Adv. Colotes* 1123a, 1124a.

So, who subverts what is commonly believed? Who wages war against what is most evident? It is those who deny that divination is possible; it is those who do not admit divine providence!

And, when does this our human life become brutish, nasty, and savage? It is when the laws are gainsaid; when the exhortations to pleasure are upheld; when divine providence is no longer believed.

U 369 = Origen, *Contra Celsum* I.13.

The Epicureans call belief in divine providence and divine omniscience superstition.

Plutarch, *Contra Epicuri Beatitud.* 1101c.

The Epicureans ridicule and slander the teaching of divine providence: they compare providence to a bugaboo that is evoked to frighten children, or to the tragic poets' Erratic Punishment which is said to be hovering over us.

On Causes

U 377* = Simplicius, On Aristotle's *Physics* B8, 198b29.

The view of certain ancient natural philosophers was that the only cause of things that come into existence is the material cause. And the Epicureans had the same view later. The mistake they were arguing against and exposing is this: that, presumably, all things are caused by intelligent choice and in accordance with a proper purpose. But it is plain for all to see that things do not happen in this fashion in nature.

U 380 = Aetius I.29.6.326D.

Epicurus defines Chance as a cause which is unstable: a) in the way it affects individuals, and b) with respect to times or places.

U 383 = Julian, *Imp. Orat.* V.162a.

Both what we call matter and something else—a form-possessing-matter—exist. But if we say that there is no cause that is prior to both of them and which precedes them in an orderly fashion, we will find ourselves unwittingly introducing the Epicurean view. To have only two first principles without anything that precedes them is to submit that everything has been put together by chance—by being randomly tossed about by itself.

U 383 = Proclus, on Plato's *Timaeus* 8off.

The Epicureans say that there is no cause in any respect which is the cause of the totality of things. . . .

But, in that case, what is the cause <and explanation of the existence> of the unlimited and eternal movement of the whole, considering that <every specific material cause> is finite and limited?

Because, as the Epicureans themselves admit, every individual body has only a finite and limited power. But, then, from what did the whole receive this power which allows it to extend and keep moving into boundless infinity <forever after?>

According to Epicurus, this shows that the power of the whole must have come about automatically and by itself—<by being inherent to the things themselves>. . . .

Nevertheless, it is Reason that is the fashioner—and god, and not Spontaneity as some claim. . . .

Because it is less likely that Epicurus' atoms would converge to one place to make a world than that nouns and verbs randomly thrown the one next to the other would ever achieve the feat of forming meaningful sentences.

Ethics

U 398 = Sextus, *Hypotyp.* III.194.

The Epicureans think that they have proved that desire is the value that is worthy to be chosen according to nature. They adduce the following as proof of this: As soon as they lapse back into their untamed state, animals impetuously plunge into pleasures and seek to avoid pain.

Sextus, *Advers. Mathem.* XI.96.

Some, who are of the Epicurean persuasion, say that, by nature, and provided that they have not been trained, animals avoid pain by might and main, and they pursue happiness.

Indeed, as soon as one is born and for as long as one is unable to restrain oneself in accordance with conventional imperatives, this is what happens <—i.e., one plunges into pursuance of pleasures and seeks to avoid pains by all means.> <For instance,> as soon as <an infant> is slapped by an unusually cold stream of air, it is always bound to cry and protest.

Since everyone is by nature bent on rushing toward pleasures impetuously and inclined to avoid pain, this proves that, according to nature, we ought to flee from pain and choose pleasure <the "ought" meant in the sense of a moral imperative.>

U 403 = Plotinus, *Enneads* II.9.

There are two views as to how to think properly about human purposes: one view posits bodily pleasure as the appropriate end-state and ultimate purpose <of human activity;> while the other view chooses the fitting goods and excellences of a human being as the values that are worthy to be chosen as proper human purposes.

By rejecting the teaching of divine providence, Epicurus inevitably exhorts us to seek after pleasure and pleasure-producing states.

U 402 = Lucianus, *Bis. Accus.* 22.
Stoic: Do you consider pain to be a moral evil?
Epicurus: Yes.
Stoic: And pleasure you consider a moral good?
Epicurus: Very much so.

U 403.35
Being atheists, the Epicureans venerated only pleasure.

U 404.6–8
If one took pleasure to be mandated by nature as the value that is worthy of choosing, then one would logically infer that pleasure is the proper moral good.

U 407 = Diogenes Laertius X.121.

The Epicureans understand happiness in two senses: one sense pertains to the supreme and highest pleasure, which has not tension whatever built into it; such is the happiness that is available to the divine. The other sense refers to the happiness that is possible by means of additions and subtractions of pleasures.

U 411 = Plutarch, *Adv. Colot.* 1122a.

Those goodly, smooth, and soothing stirrings of the flesh invite us—and this we know without prior instruction. This is what the Epicureans say. Even he who denies and disowns them is still swayed and softened by pleasures.

U 416 = Olympiodorus, on Plato's *Philebus* 274.

Epicurus says that, by nature, pleasure is a static of static equilibrium.

U 417 = Plutarch, *Contra Epicuri Beat.* 1086e.

Epicurus says that all types of pleasures are actually similar to each other and that they depend on the same mechanism: They have an end and proper limit at the point at which everything that was painful has been removed. As if nature were to allow for an increase in the feeling of pleasure only up to, but never beyond, the point the painful is cancelled out and is felt no longer—except for certain unnecessary variants of pleasure which are admitted even when they are not needed for the relief of pain.

The time it takes for the appetite to reach that point is the standard by which we measure pleasures; and, therefore, pleasures are actually short-lived both in their combined effects and taken each one individually.

Nevertheless, the Epicureans realized that this teaching is really too stinting and decided to transfer the field of the objectives of pleasure-seeking from the body—a wretchedly barren field—to the soul where they expected to find meadows and crops brimming on all sides with grand pleasures. . . .

Don't you think that they did well and right by starting with the body, which usually feels the first manifestations, and then transferring the seat of pleasure to the soul—as to a more secure place? In this way even the Epicureans were essentially admitting that everything finds its proper purpose and perfection in the soul!

U 425 = Epictetus, fragment 52.

How is it possible that, as Epicurus says, the soul rejoices and waxes tranquil by having bodily goods, which are less weighty, and yet the soul does not find pleasure in its own proper goods, which are far greater?

U 442

It is better that we endure certain pains, so that we will be able to derive even greater satisfaction from the pleasures.

And it is to our interest to refrain from certain pleasures so that we don't get to suffer from pains which feel even greater than they really are.

U 469

Thanks be to blessed Nature—that she has made necessities easy to provide for and that she made what is difficult to provide unnecessary.

U 485 = Porphyry, *Ad Marcellam* 29.

One can become wretchedly unhappy either from fear <of invisible things> or because of pointless desire which remains without satisfaction.

And yet it is possible to make oneself happy by using reason in order to prevail over such nuisances.

U 488 = *Gnomologion* (Parisian Code 1168f.115)

The poor soul is usually stupefied into inanity by good times and is annihilated by adversity.

U 489 = Porphyry, *Ad Marcellam* 30.

Both reason and nature teach us to attach less significance to vagaries of fortune; and, when we are in happy times, to know and mark well that this too is tantamount to having bad luck; and, when, on the other hand, we are in bad luck, that we should not worry because we should not attach much importance to being happy anyway; and to accept the goods that come to us from fortune without making much ado about them; and to always put side by side in our mind the presumed good things next to those which are naturally considered bad; and, as for what the masses take to be good, we should consider that to be actually bad and ephemeral; and that wisdom holds no intercourse with luck or chance.

U 504 = Diogenes Laertius X.138.

According to Epicurus, the virtues are worthy to be chosen not for their own sake—as is the case with a healthy regimen and with health itself—but only for the sake of the pleasures which they are bound to produce.

U 519 = Clement of Alexandria, *Stromateis* VI.2.

The most important result of practicing justice is peace of mind. This is what Epicurus says commenting on a text that reads as follows: "If you be just, you are to have a stable life for evermore; and this is a good life, which you can then lead—one without tormenting fears or vexing disturbances."

On Human Society

U 524 = Plutarch, *On the Uses of Oracles* 1129b.

If one praises god and justice and admits providence in his study of nature; and if he applauds law-abidingness and welcomes human society and government, and not utility, in his study of ethics: why would such a person ever care to withdraw from society and live a life concealed from scrutiny <as the Epicureans practice?>

U 523 = Arrian, *Epict. Disc.* II.20.6.20.20.

When Epicurus wants to refute the claim that human sociability is by nature, he contradicts himself by using as premise that which he purports to prove. Because, see what he is saying: Don't be deceived, good people; don't let yourselves be led astray and don't fall into error; because, mind you, there is no natural sociability among rational creatures—nothing by nature which compels them to be sociable. Those who tell you otherwise are being absurd and are trying to hoodwink you.

In this way Epicurus rejects all those virile vocations that one can have in his capacity as host, citizen, or friend; but Epicurus is not rejecting—indeed, he cannot possibly reject—the claim that there are certain distinctly human propensities.[1]

U 526 = Clement, *Stromateis* II.2.3.

Democritus removes marriage and the begetting of children from the class of necessary pleasures on the grounds that they are filled with nuisance and onerous burdens. And Epicurus sides with Democritus on this—and so do all those who posit that the good consists in pleasure, peace of mind, and in the complete absence of sadness.

U 540 = Diogenes Laertius X.120.

Epicurus thinks that friendships are formed ultimately out of considerations of utility. Because one must think ahead and act in the present for the sake of future benefit—as we do, for instance, when we sow seed into the soil. And, Epicurus says, once formed, friendship makes possible the most intense social pleasures.

U 543 = Diogenes Laertius X.11.

Diocles says that Epicurus did not request that possessions be set aside and placed into a common trough—contrary to what Pythagoras had asked when he said that "friends have everything in common." <Epicurus' rejoinder to this was that such a practice> would actually betoken mutual. . .distrust. And, if they distrust each other, then they are no friends in the first place.

U 548

Happiness and a blessed state do not depend on having a lot of money or on the volume of one's possessions; not even on having political power or being in high office. They rather consist in the absence of sadness and in the mild character of one's passions and in the disposition of a soul that sets goals in accordance with nature.

ENDNOTES

INTRODUCTION

[1] To avoid an ancient problem, Newton took empty space to be "something" rather than nothing. On the other hand, Epicurus' space or "nothingness" (*to kenon*) might be an absence rather than a substance. But this is not entirely clear given that Epicurus states that the void *exists*. Nevertheless, similar problems beset the two notions.

EPICURUS,
LETTER TO MENEOCEUS

[1] Theognis, 425–427.

EPICURUS,
SHORT FRAGMENTS AND TESTIMONIA
(UNCERTAIN AUTHENTICITY)

[1] The contradiction consists in that Epicurus appeals to his followers as friends and exhorts them in the name of friendship whereas, if human beings are not sociable, there is no ground, in Epicurus' naturalist ethics, for justifying or practicing friendship in the first place.

INDEX

Absolute:
Absolute Beginning of All Motions: 6.
Absolute Space: xix; see also Newton, Newtonian.
Absolute Orientation in Space: 15.
Accident (s): xxi, xxii, 20, 72.
Accidental Properties, Accidental Attributes: 4, 9; see also Incidental Properties.
Action (s): xviii, xxiii, 26, 54, 60; see also Voluntary Action.
Admixture: 17, 42, 72; see also Mixture.
Aetius: 65, 71, 74, 76, 77, 78, 80, 82
Affects: 9, 11, 12, 19, 22, 23, 52, 65, 72, 76, 82 see also Emotions.
Afterlife: xiii, xxi, 26, 59.
Air: 9, 10, 11, 34, 37, 39, 40, 42, 43, 44, 67, 75, 76, 77, 79, 84.
Alexander Aphrodisias: 73, 77.
Anguish: x, xiv, 26; see also Distress, Disturbance, Perturbation.
Animals: xxiv, 22, 37, 46, 55, 60, 83.
Annihilation: 86; see also Destruction.
Anthropic Principle: xx.
Appearance (s): xviii, 7, 8, 12, 25, 30, 31, 34, 37, 38, 43, 44, 67, 70, 77.
Aristotelian, Aristotelianism: xvi, xxv, 71.
Aristotle: vii, ix, xxv, 71, 73, 77, 78, 82.
Astrology: 45.
Atheism, Atheists: vii, xiv, 84.

Athens: vii, xi.
Atom (s): xvii, xiii, xix, xx, xxi, xxii, xxiii, xxiv, 4, 5, 6, 7, 8, 9, 11, 12, 13, 14, 15, 16, 18, 30, 32, 38, 39, 71.
Atomic Properties: xviii, xix, xx, 6, 12; see also Shape, Size, Mass.
Atomic Theory: ix, xvi, xvii, xviii, xix, 71; see also Atomism, Atomists.
Atomic Types: xix, xx, xxi, 32, 71.
Atomism, Atomists: ix, xiv, xvii.
Attributes: 4, 11, 12, 14, 19, 20, 26, 45; see also Accidental Attributes, Properties.
Avoidance: xxiv, xxv, 21, 52, 54, 63, 83.

Bad (moral sense): xxii, 50, 54, 55, 57, 61, 86.
Bad Judgment: 55.
Bad Life: xxii.
Bad Luck: 55, 81, 86.
Basic:
Basic Affections: 65.
Basic Entity: xvii.
Basic Principles: xix.
Basic Property: 74.
Blaze: 33, 46; see also Conflagration, Fire, Flames.
Blessed, Blessedness: 24, 25, 26, 29, 30, 36, 46, 49, 52, 54, 56, 60, 80, 81, 86, 88.

SUGGESTED READING

ASMIS, ELIZABETH. *Epicurus' Scientific Method.* Ithaca, NY: Cornell University Press, 1984.

BAILEY, CYRIL. *The Greek Atomists and Epicurus.* Oxford: Clarendon, 1928.

BAILEY, CYRIL, ED. AND TRANS. *Epicurus: The Extant Remains.* Oxford: Clarendon, 1926.

DEWITT, NORMAN. *Epicurus and His Philosophy.* Minneapolis, MN: University of Minnesota Press, 1954.

ENGLERT, WALTER. *Epicurus on the Swerve and Involuntary Action.* Atlanta, GA: Scholars Press, 1987.

FESTUGIERE, A. J. *Epicurus and His Gods.* Trans. C. W. Chilton. Oxford: Blackwell, 1955.

FURLEY, D. *Two Studies of Greek Atomists.* Princeton: Princeton University Press, 1967.

HICKS, R. D. *Stoic and Epicurean.* New York: Scribner, 1910.

JONES, HOWARD. *The Epicurean Tradition.* New York: Routledge, 1989.

KONSTAN, DAVID. *Some Aspects of Epicurean Psychology.* Leiden: Brill, 1973.

LUCRETIUS. *De Rerun Natura.* Trans. W. H. D. Rouse. Ed. M. F. Smith. Cambridge, MA: Harvard University Press, 1975.

MITSIS, PHILLIP. *Epicurus' Ethical Theory: The Pleasures of Invulnerability.* Ithaca, NY: Cornell University Press, 1988.

PANICHAS, GEORGE. *Epicurus.* New York: Twayne, 1967.

PYLE, ANDREW. *Atomism and Its Critics.* Bristol, U.K.: Thoemmes, 1995.

RIST, J. M. *Epicurus: An Introduction.* Cambridge: Cambridge University Press, 1972.

STRAUSS, LEO. *Natural Right and History.* Chicago: Chicago University Press, 1953.

TAYLOR, A. E. *Epicurus.* London: Constable, 1911.

USENER, H., ED. *Epicurea.* Leibzig: Teubner, 1887.

ZELLER, EDUARD. *The Stoics, Epicureans, and Skeptics.* O. J. Reichel. London: Longmans, 1880.